Cook

Coøk

by Mikkel Karstad

photographer Anders Schønnemann

CLEARVIEW

I've worked with many chefs over the years, and there was no question that I was in the presence of someone very special when I met Mikkel Karstad in November 2005. At the time, I had just accepted an offer to write and front 13 episodes of a new TV series, *New Scandinavian Cooking*, which was being distributed globally. I needed a wingman; Mikkel had applied and got the job.

Over the following year, we travelled throughout Denmark with detours to Greenland and Norway. We researched and created our recipes together, decided whom to interview, how the visuals should work and co-wrote the episode manuscripts. We cooked in the freezing cold (raw shrimps in buttermilk foam in –20° C in the Disco Bay), and in the searing heat (fishcakes in +32° C in the sand dunes of the Skaw). Wherever we went, we had fun with our crew as well as our local friends and hosts, and, while we missed homes and families, most nights we went to sleep with huge grins on our faces, satisfied with our day's work and achievements.

Mikkel was an excellent travel companion. Always helpful and always one step ahead, never once did he lose his sharp focus. On several occasions, it was Mikkel and not the soundman, the editor or the photographers who noticed I'd got something wrong. And when everyone else was convinced that it was a wrap, I'd often hear Mikkel's voice: 'Claus, you said this and this … or you did that and that … are you okay with it?' Usually I wouldn't be, and then we'd have to shoot the scene again!

Once we'd finished shooting *The Taste of Denmark* (as the series became known), Mikkel helped me start up Meyer's Deli in Magasin, a major department store in Copenhagen. After that he became gastronomic advisor to Meyer's Food House until 2008, when I persuaded him to help me finish a marathon project, which two years later became the cookbook, *Almanac*. The completion of the *Almanac* project would not have run so smoothly, had we not shared so many previous experiences and through them gained such detailed knowledge of our professional and human strengths and weaknesses as well as our needs and values. I gained terrific respect for Mikkel both personally and professionally and I always felt completely at ease working with him (which I believe is reciprocated) as we synchronised our ideas about how to present the food, in terms of both taste and appearance.

But it wasn't all TV and recipes. Among the many experiences Mikkel and I have shared, I particularly recall eating raw seal's liver on an ice floe in the middle of the sea outside Illulissat, roasting freshly shot grouse in Motunheimen National Park, the spread of cakes in Southern Jutland and the magnificent oysters we enjoyed at the Liim Fiord.

I remember the times we went swimming together in remote lakes, the times we went running together, and the extraordinary time when Mikkel served 10 different sample dishes to 150 visitors in an hour and a half, all on his own, in a kitchen without water or electricity, while I was giving the talk that he created the tastes for.

Mikkel, our collaboration ended in 2011, when you took the position as head chef at Horton, the prestigious law firm. Here you not only won the 2012 Canteen Prize, but also continued producing recipes and food photography for I don't know how many magazines, and never neglected your beloved family.

I have a feeling that our paths will cross again one day, but maybe that's just wishful thinking. And so, if they don't, I just want to tell you: Damn, I've learnt a lot from you Mikkel, and it was always such a pleasure.

Thank you so much for the journey.

Claus Meyer

Having spent many years in different kitchens – restaurant kitchens, large kitchens, small kitchens, outdoor kitchens, home kitchens and other people's kitchens – and having produced recipes for other people's books, I've now been given the opportunity to create my own cookbook based on some of the wonderful raw ingredients I value the most.

I hope that you'll use my recipes as they are, but also be inspired to choose a main ingredient, such as octopus or offal, and then improvise using what's available and in season at that time.

A recipe such as the broccoli soup with octopus, garlic and verbena (see p. 48) is lovely in summer when broccoli is at its best. However, in winter when you feel like making a soup to go with your fresh octopus, you can of course opt for frozen broccoli, or buy a beautiful, large stalk of curly kale and make an equally lovely soup with that.

Regardless of whether you slavishly follow my recipes or decide to improvise through trial and error, the book, and my thoughts behind it, will come into its own as long as you produce wonderful, homemade food to be enjoyed in the company of friends and family.

Have fun!

Mikkel Karstad

Find more recipes and food videos at my blog
weyoutheyate.com

FIRE

I love cooking over an open fire as it combines beauty, good times and great tastes.

Cooking over flames can be a little tricky in terms of control, but it adds that strong smoky flavour, which is almost impossible to obtain when using a grill pan or barbecue, be it coal or gas-fired.

If you have some firewood to hand, use your barbecue or the designated fireplace to light it in a proper boy or girl-scout fashion, using newspaper and twigs to get it going. Then you'll be certain to get that pure, authentic taste of open fire cooking.

N 55° 59.183'
E 12° 33.269'

Chargrilled pointed cabbage

4 people

200 g cleaned chanterelles
100 ml good olive oil
sea salt
freshly ground pepper
2 pointed cabbages
4 spring onions with stalks
1 bunch of flat leaf parsley
500 ml cider vinegar

Clean the chanterelles and cut them into smaller pieces if they are very big.

Roast the chanterelles in a little olive oil on a pan, either directly over the barbecue or open fire, for 2–3 minutes to give them a nice colour and to soften them a little. Add salt and pepper and then take the pan off the heat.

Remove the roughest of the outer cabbage leaves and slice each cabbage along, into 8 equally sized pieces, leaving a little of the stalk on each, which will hold the pieces together.

Drizzle a little olive oil over the cabbage and sear on a very hot barbecue for 2–3 minutes on each side, which will give the surface that distinctive chargrilled look.

Remove the cabbage from the grill and place in a dish. Sprinkle the warm chanterelles over the cabbage.

Top and tail the onions and remove the outer layer if necessary. Slice them thinly and sprinkle the rings over the cabbage and chanterelles.

Finally, add some chopped parsley, olive oil, cider vinegar, salt and freshly ground pepper.

Serve the warm cabbage and chanterelles as a side dish with meat, e.g. hanger steak on page 24. On its own, you can also serve it as a lunch salad or a vegetarian dish as part of a larger menu.

Aubergine mash

4 people

2 aubergines
50 ml good olive oil
1 unwaxed lemon
½ garlic clove
sea salt
freshly ground pepper

Place the aubergines directly in the embers and leave them there for approx. 30 minutes, after which they should be burnt on the outside and soft on the inside.

Remove the aubergines and halve them.

Scrape out the flesh and place in a sieve, allowing the moisture to drip away.

Chop the aubergine flesh with a knife, place it in a bowl, and add olive oil, finely grated lemon zest and lemon juice, finely chopped garlic, salt and freshly ground pepper. Once mixed through, the aubergine will mash naturally.

Serve it in a bowl as a side dish with meat, e.g. hanger steak on page 24, or as a small snack on a slice of bread.

Hay-grilled langoustine

4 people

12 langoustines
1 handful hay
10 mint stalks
½ cucumber
40 g fresh de-stalked redcurrants
1 unwaxed lemon
100 ml good olive oil
1 tsp. liquid honey
5 thyme sprigs
sea salt
freshly ground pepper

Place the langoustines in an ovenproof dish and wrap them well in hay and mint.

Place the langoustines directly on the barbecue and leave there for 3–4 minutes, allowing the hay and mint to be almost completely consumed by the flames, adding a lovely smoked and perfumed flavour to the langoustines.

Peel the cucumber and dice it finely. Put the cucumber dice in a bowl with redcurrants, finely grated lemon zest and lemon juice, olive oil, honey, chopped thyme, salt and freshly ground pepper. Mix well for a thick dressing.

Remove the langoustines from the barbecue and place in a dish. Serve them as they are, allowing your guests to shell them themselves, with some good bread and the dressing.

Depending on your mood, you can also choose to shell the langoustines and serve them on a plate, doused in dressing.

Grilled hanger steak

WITH A WARM DRESSING OF MARROW, TARRAGON, RED ONIONS AND CAPERS

DRESSING

50 g marrow extracted from pipe cut marrow bones (ask your butcher to do this for you)
2 red onions
50 g capers
100 ml good olive oil
50 ml sherry vinegar
sea salt
freshly ground pepper
1 bunch of tarragon

Dice the marrow finely. Peel the red onions, then halve and slice finely.

Chop the capers and put everything into an old saucepan, able to withstand the heat of the barbecue (or prepare the dressing in the kitchen).

Add oil, vinegar, salt and pepper to the saucepan and place it on the barbecue. Heat it carefully until the marrow starts to melt and it all 'boils' down to a thick dressing.

Chop the tarragon and add to the warm dressing.

Pour the dressing over the cooked slices of meat and serve immediately.

If you leave meat and dressing for too long before serving, the marrow and dressing will 'settle' and thus become too fatty.

4 people

Trim the hanger steaks, removing the membranes and excess fat, but make sure to leave a little fat, as it adds flavour to the meat. Put the steaks in a bowl and rub them with thyme, garlic, olive oil, salt and freshly ground pepper.

Leave the steaks to marinate for 15–20 minutes before grilling them over an open fire, giving them the full works for a short while, approx. 4–5 minutes (depending on thickness) on each side. This will give the steaks a nicely browned crust while leaving them succulent and pink in the middle. It's important not to grill a hanger steak for too long as it has a fairly coarse structure, which can turn hard and tough if overcooked. However, when properly cooked, the meat is very succulent and tasty.

Remove the hanger steaks from the barbecue and leave them to settle for 5–7 minutes, before slicing finely and serving along with the warm dressing.

If you're unable to get hold of hanger steaks, you can use rump or sirloin steak instead.

800 g – 1 kg hanger steaks
5 thyme or rosemary sprigs
2 garlic cloves
some good olive oil
sea salt
freshly ground pepper

Flambéed strawberries

4 people

Wash and hull the strawberries. Leave them to drain.

Heat a frying pan directly on the embers and add honey. Once the honey starts to sizzle and caramelize, add the strawberries. Leave the strawberries to 'fry' for 30 seconds, then add the dog rose petals as well as the finely grated lime zest and lime juice and leave for another minute, until it thickens and turns into a light syrup.

Add whisky (as much as you like) before tilting the frying pan a little and shaking it, allowing the flames to catch the alcohol and flambé the strawberries. Once the alcohol has caught fire, shake the pan gently, until the flames die out and the alcohol has evaporated. Add the verbena leaves and shake the frying pan once more.

Serve the strawberries immediately, directly off the frying pan, while they're warm, and add a generous dollop of strawberry sorbet.

You can also make this dessert with other fruits and berries, including peaches, apricots, plums, pears and apples.

500 g fresh strawberries
1 litre of water
200 g cane sugar
½ vanilla pod
10 whole black peppercorns
2 unwaxed lemons

500 g strawberries
2 tbsp. liquid honey
1 small handful of dog rose petals
1 small handful of verbena leaves
1 unwaxed lime
1 small drop of whisky

STRAWBERRY SORBET

Wash and hull the strawberries. Leave them to drain.

Halve the strawberries and put them in a saucepan with water, vanilla seeds, sugar and the whole black peppercorns. The peppercorns help 'cut' the sweetness of the sorbet, enhancing the flavour of the strawberries.

Bring to the boil and leave for 3–4 minutes. Take the saucepan off the heat and flavour with finely grated lemon zest and lemon juice. Leave the strawberry mixture for 20 minutes.

Blend the mixture to a purée and strain through a coarse-meshed sieve, allowing a little of the strawberry pulp to push through. Place the strawberry purée in the fridge to cool down.

Once the sorbet pickle is completely cold, pour into an ice cream maker and turn to sorbet. Place the finished sorbet in a plastic container and leave in the freezer. The sorbet can be left in a freezer for up to 3–4 days without losing its lovely, creamy texture.

FENNEL

With its strong anise scent and liquorice flavour, some people find fennel too overpowering. Personally, I'm a great fan of this perfumed vegetable.

I like it raw in salads, fried, grilled, baked and braised, in soups and even in desserts and ice cream. Fennel can be used for almost anything.

Growing your own fennel is fairly simple, and that way you can make the most of top and root, both highly suitable for eating. If you don't have a garden where you can grow your own, you can buy fennel almost anywhere – well, the root at least. So start using some fennel – it tastes great!

Crunchy fennel salad

WITH KOHLRABI, DILL, MUSTARD AND RYE BREAD

CRISPY RYE BREAD

¼ of a day-old loaf of
rye bread
2–3 tbsp. good olive oil
sea salt

Slice the rye bread finely. Using rye bread that's a little dry is your best bet, but you can also leave the bread in the freezer for a little while, which will make it easier to slice.

Place the slices on a baking sheet with baking paper. Drizzle some olive oil on top and then sprinkle with sea salt. Bake in the oven for 8–10 minutes at 180°, until crispy and golden.

Take the rye bread out of the oven and leave to cool. This will make it really crispy.

The crispy rye bread slices will keep for as long as 2–3 weeks in an airtight container or a glass jar.

You can also use these crispy slices of rye bread as chips for the children or a little pre-dinner snack.

4–6 people

Top and tail the fennel bulbs and thinly slice them, using either a mandolin or a very sharp knife – but be careful, don't cut your fingers!

Peel the kohlrabi and slice it finely on mandolin or with a sharp knife.

Put the fennel and kohlrabi in a bowl with cold water and leave for a bit as this enhances the crunchiness of both vegetables, which is perfect for this salad.

Mix curd, vinegar, oil, honey, salt, pepper and mustard into a dressing.

Drain the fennel and kohlrabi well and mix in with the dressing.

Sprinkle some dill and crispy rye bread on top and serve immediately. If you leave the salad it may collapse, as the dressing softens those thin slices of fennel and kohlrabi.

You can serve the salad on its own for lunch or as a side dish with fish or poultry. Try serving it with a fried fillet of fish, fried herring or fish cakes – it works really well!

2 fennel bulbs
1 kohlrabi
3 tbsp. curd or natural yoghurt
3 tbsp. cider vinegar
2 tbsp. good olive or rapeseed oil
1 tsp. liquid honey
sea salt
freshly ground pepper
1 tbsp. coarse mustard
½ bunch of dill
crispy rye bread

Fennel risotto

4 people

Peel and dice the shallot, and one fennel bulb. Sauté in 10 g butter, until clear and soft but not brown. When making risotto, you should always use a good, thick-bottomed saucepan, to make sure the rice won't burn.

Add the rice and leave it to sauté for a little before adding the wine, which should be completely reduced and evaporated before moving on to adding the stock.

Bring water or vegetable stock to the boil in a separate saucepan, and keep it boiling. Add boiling water to the rice a little at a time, keeping the rice constantly covered. Stir continuously to ensure that the rice won't stick to the bottom of the saucepan.

Cook the rice for 15–18 minutes, until it's soft yet still retains a bite. It's important to add salt while cooking, which will allow the rice to absorb the salt.

Meanwhile, you can shell the langoustines. Make sure you remove the intestine.

Finely slice the remaining fennel bulb, rinse in cold water, and drain thoroughly. Gently mix together the fennel, coarsely chopped chervil and leaves of garden sorrel, a little cider vinegar, olive oil, salt and pepper. Set aside.

Take the rice off the heat, and then add the remaining dollop of butter, the mascarpone and the Parmesan cheese, giving the risotto a creamy and almost liquid consistency. Add salt, pepper and vinegar to taste.

Heat a frying pan and fry the langoustine tails at strong heat for approx. 30 seconds on each side, giving them a nicely fried crust while remaining succulent in the centre. Then remove from the heat and keep ready for serving on top of the risotto.

Serve the risotto in deep dishes. Place the langoustine tails and the fennel salad on top and eat immediately. It's important to eat the risotto straight away, because if you leave it, the rice will absorb the moisture and become overcooked, sticky and dull.

1 shallot
2 fennel bulbs
25 g butter
300 g risotto rice
100 ml white wine
1 litre of water or vegetable stock
8 langoustines
½ bunch of chervil
10 garden sorrel leaves
2–3 tbsp. good olive oil
sea salt
freshly ground pepper
3 tbsp. mascarpone
40 g grated Parmesan

Grilled fennel

4 people

1 red onion
3–4 tbsp. cider vinegar
1 tsp. liquid honey
sea salt
freshly ground pepper
2 fennel bulbs
3–4 tbsp. good olive oil
4 fresh chorizo sausages for frying
½ bunch of basil

Peel the red onion and halve, then finely slice into strips.

Add onion strips to a bowl and marinate in vinegar, honey, a little salt and freshly ground pepper. Leave for 15–20 minutes, which will allow the onion slices to soften and lose a little of the tangy onion flavour, while retaining their crunchiness.

Top and tail the fennel bulbs – it's important to leave a little of the root intact, as it will hold the slices together once you start cutting it. Cut the fennel lengthways, into 8 pieces.

Toss the fennel pieces in some olive oil, salt and pepper and then grill them under a hot grill or on a grill pan for approx. 2–3 minutes on each side, which will leave those beautiful, grilled stripes and a slightly charred surface.

Grill the sausages for a few minutes, ensuring they are thoroughly cooked, while also giving them a robust, scorched look.

Remove both fennel and sausages from the grill and serve in a dish or on a plate alongside the marinated onions, sprinkling lots of coarsely chopped basil on top.

Serve the grilled fennel as a light lunch dish, as part of a larger barbecue menu or as a side order with grilled chicken.

You can also make this dish without the sausages, using courgettes, aubergines, capsicums or tomatoes instead.

Pickled fennel

CRISPBREAD WITH FENNEL SEEDS AND SEA SALT

50 g polenta (maize flakes)
200 ml semi-skimmed milk
15 g fennel seeds
220 g wheat flour
coarse sea salt

Add polenta and milk to a bowl.

Roast the fennel seeds on a dry frying pan, until they start to pop, then crush them in a mortar. Add half to the bowl with polenta and milk, save the rest for sprinkling on top of the crispbread. Leave the fennel and polenta mix on the kitchen table for 10 minutes.

Add flour to the fennel and polenta mix, a little at a time, until the dough is smooth (save a little flour for rolling out the dough). Leave the dough in the fridge for 15 minutes.

Divide the dough into 6–8 portions and roll them into big, very thin flakes on a kitchen table just lightly covered in flour. Place the flakes on a baking sheet with baking paper.

1 preserving jar of ½ litre

Top and tail the fennel bulbs, then halve and finely slice them.

Put the fennel, vinegar, sugar, star anise, a little salt and freshly ground pepper into a saucepan.

Bring to the boil and cook for 15–20 minutes on low heat, which will turn the fennel into a thick compote, but don't overdo it, as it's important to retain some of the vegetable's shape.

Take the saucepan off the heat and leave the fennel compote to cool. Add sugar, vinegar, salt and pepper to taste, balancing sweetness and acidity.

Pour the warm fennel compote into a preserving jar and close the lid.

Unopened, the compote will keep for 30–45 days in the fridge. When opened, it will keep for 10–15 days.

Brush the crispbreads with a little water and then sprinkle sea salt and fennel seeds on top.

Bake the crispbreads in the oven for 6–8 minutes at 170°, until golden and crispy.

Leave the crispbreads to cool and serve with cheese and compote. You can also place the crispbreads in an airtight container, where they'll keep for longer.

3 fennel bulbs
200 ml cider vinegar
100 ml cane sugar
1 star anise
sea salt
ground pepper

Fennel and pear sorbet

WITH GRAPPA
AND DRIED PEARS

4–6 people

Add water, sugar, glucose and fennel seeds to a saucepan and bring to the boil.

Chop fennel and pears into smaller pieces – no need to peel the pears.

Add fennel and pears to the hot sugar pickle and leave to boil for 10–15 minutes over low heat.

Take the saucepan off the heat and pour pears, fennel and sugar pickle into a liquidizer and blend until fairly smooth.

Sift the pulp through a coarse sieve, leaving it completely smooth, but allow a little of the fruity pulp to go through and then add pear vinegar and grappa to taste. Place the sorbet in the fridge and leave to cool.

Once the sorbet is completely cold, pour into an ice cream maker and turn to sorbet. Put the finished sorbet in a bowl or plastic container, place in the freezer, allowing it to settle completely before serving.

Serve the sorbet with crispy, dried pears and a little wood sorrel or lemon balm on top. The sorbet can be served as a dessert in its own right but it also works great as accompaniment to heavy chocolate cake or any other heavy cake or dessert, as the sorbet adds a really fresh touch.

½ litre of water
180 g sugar
40 g glucose syrup
15 fennel seeds
1 fennel bulb
500 g ripe pears
2–3 tbsp. pear vinegar
25 ml grappa

DRIED PEARS
2 pears

Slice the whole pears very thinly, using a mandolin or a very sharp knife.

Place the pear slices on a piece of baking paper on a baking sheet and dry in the oven until crispy, 2½–3 hours at 60° (hot air) – and remember to leave the oven door ajar.

The dried pears will keep for a long time if stored in an airtight container.

OCTOPUS

Some of my absolute favourite foods are octopus and squid, and fortunately, it's rubbed off on my family.

When we're on holiday, we eat octopus and squid until they're coming out our ears. And we also indulge when we can get fresh squid in Denmark. Unfortunately though, octopuses can't survive in my native waters.

You can buy the best squid in late spring and early autumn. It should be fresh, firm and smell and look good. And it's very important that you prepare it carefully.

If you treat squid and octopus the wrong way, i.e. cook them for too long over low heat, they will turn hard, tough and dry. But if you treat them right, they're pure bliss. Undervalued but healthy, tasty and tender.

Grilled octopus

FRIED TOMATOES

8 different coloured tomatoes
4 fresh elderflower heads, stalks trimmed
50 ml dog rose vinegar
1 tbsp. honey
10 thyme sprigs
4 shallots
4 tbsp. good olive oil
sea salt
freshly ground pepper

Rinse the tomatoes, and cut in half. Place on a dry frying pan, cut side down, and fry for 2–3 minutes, which will give them a good colour and crust.

Cut (using scissors) the elderflowers from their remaining stalks and add them to the frying pan with the tomatoes. Then add vinegar, honey, thyme and the thinly sliced shallots. Leave tomatoes to fry for another minute, until they have absorbed the vinegar.

Sprinkle salt and pepper on the tomatoes before taking the frying pan off the heat and adding the remaining olive oil. Cover the tomatoes thoroughly in the warm vinaigrette and serve in a dish while still warm.

4 people

Rinse the octopus in cold water and then place it in a saucepan. Cover in cold water and add salt as well as coarsely chopped carrot, onion and garlic.

Bring to the boil and then leave octopus to simmer for approx. 45 minutes. Turn off the heat and leave to settle in the water for another 30–40 minutes. You want the octopus to be tender while also retaining a little bite.

Take the octopus from the saucepan and chop into smaller pieces. Marinate the pieces in garlic, olive oil and freshly chopped rosemary.

Place the octopus pieces on a barbecue or a hot grill pan and cook for 2–3 minutes before turning them over and giving them another 2–3 minutes, which will give them a nice crust and a great charred taste.

Remove the octopus pieces from the barbecue or grill pan, sprinkle with sea salt and serve immediately with fried tomatoes.

1 octopus weighing approx. 1 kg
coarse salt
1 carrot
1 onion
1 garlic clove
some finely chopped garlic
some good olive oil
1 sprig of fresh rosemary
sea salt
freshly ground pepper

Broccoli soup

4 people

1 head of broccoli
1 shallot
1 garlic clove
¼ fresh red seedless chilli
2 tbsp. good olive oil
sea salt
freshly ground pepper
½ litre of water
200 g cleaned squid (see page 53)
2 verbena sprigs
(use lemon balm, mint, tarragon
or chervil as an alternative)

Divide the broccoli into small pieces and rinse in cold water (you can use it all, including the stalk). Put a couple of florets to one side and chop finely as garnish.

Peel the shallot and the garlic clove and chop coarsely. Then add onion, garlic and chilli to a saucepan and sauté gently in 1 tbsp. olive oil for 1 minute, making sure the onion doesn't brown. Add broccoli, salt and pepper and sauté for another minute. Add boiling water and leave to cook for 5 minutes. While the soup is bubbling, you can prepare the squid (see how to clean it on page 53).

Cut the squid into smaller pieces and add to a bowl before tossing in a little olive oil. Then fry the squid on a hot frying pan for approx. 30 seconds, giving them only a short, sharp fry-up, which will allow them to maintain their moisture and their softness. If you fry the squid for too long or if you fry it over low heat, it'll start to 'boil' on the frying pan, which will make it dry and tough. Remove the squid from the frying pan and sprinkle the pieces with salt and pepper. Then mix with the finely chopped broccoli from earlier.

Blend the soup immediately and add salt and pepper while gently re-heating it. Serve with the fried squid and raw broccoli and sprinkle verbena on top to give it a fresh and citrusy flavour. Serve good bread with the soup as a starter or a light lunch.

It's important that you keep within the designated time for cooking this dish, ensuring that you don't boil the soup after you've blended it, because then it'll lose its colour and freshness.

Octopus Salad

*with pearl barley, chilli
and radicchio*

Fried Squid
on grilled bread with cream cheese or fresh goat's cheese, asparagus and basil

Octopus salad

4–6 people

Rinse the octopus in cold water and then place it in a saucepan. Cover in cold water and then add salt as well as coarsely chopped carrot, onion and garlic.

Bring to the boil and leave the octopus to simmer for approx. 45 minutes. Then turn off the heat and leave to settle in the brine for another 30–40 minutes. You want the octopus to be tender, but with a little bite to it. Leave the octopus to cool down in the brine.

Put the pearl barley in a saucepan and cover in water. Cook for 35–40 minutes, or until the barley softens. Take the saucepan off the heat and drain excess water before pouring the pearl barley into a bowl. Marinate in oil, salt, freshly ground pepper, honey and finely grated lemon zest and lemon juice, while it is still warm. Toss well. Leave the pearl barley to cool.

Remove the seeds from the chilli before slicing finely. Tear the radicchio into small pieces, rinse in water and drain. Add the radicchio and chilli to the pearl barley.

1 octopus (approx. 1 kg)
1 carrot
1 onion
1 garlic clove
coarse salt
100 g pearl barley
4 tbsp. olive oil
sea salt
freshly ground pepper
1 tsp. liquid honey
1 unwaxed lemon
½ fresh red chilli
1 radicchio
1 bunch of chervil

Chop the octopus into smaller bits and add to the salad. Toss everything well, and add salt, pepper and lemon to taste.

Chop the chervil coarsely and sprinkle on top.

Serve the octopus salad as a lunch dish in its own right or as part of a main meal. You can also serve it with fried squid on grilled bread as a starter (see opposite page).

Fried squid

4–6 people

Clean the squid in cold water by pulling its head/arms from its body. Pull the thin membrane from its body and rinse the body thoroughly with cold water – there can be quite a bit of goo inside. Pull the 2–3 long, transparent 'ribs' from the body and throw them out. You can now finely slice the body. Rinse the arms in cold water and sever the stomach from right above the eyes. Throw the stomach out. Cut the arms into smaller pieces and the body into strips.

Put the pieces of squid in a bowl and marinate in a little olive oil and garlic.

Break off the woody ends of the asparagus and throw these away. Rinse the asparagus and cut in two, lengthways. Bring a saucepan with lightly salted water to the boil and blanch the asparagus for 1–2 minutes, depending on thickness. Then immediately place in cold water, which will help maintain its crunchiness and colour.

Dip the slices of bread in olive oil and grill on a hot grill pan or under the oven grill, giving them a golden, crispy texture.

Remove the bread slices from the grill pan and spread fresh cheese on them. Place the asparagus halves and basil on top.

1 squid weighing approx. 500g
1 garlic clove, finely chopped
50 ml good olive oil, approx.
8–12 green asparagus
50 g fresh cream cheese or goat's cheese
½ bunch of basil
2 tbsp. cider vinegar
sea salt
freshly ground pepper

Fry the pieces of squid in olive oil, on a very hot frying pan, for approx. 30 seconds, giving them only a short, sharp fry-up, which will ensure that they retain their moisture and softness. If you fry the squid for too long or if you fry it over low heat, it'll start to 'boil' on the frying pan, and it will turn dry and tough. If you have a lot of squid to cook, fry it in several batches rather than all at once, because if you put too much on the frying pan it will lose heat and then the squid will not be cooked properly.

Grilled octopus

WITH SPLIT PEA PURÉE, ALMONDS, YOGHURT AND CHARGRILLED LEMON

SPLIT PEA PURÉE

100 g split peas
1 garlic clove
100 ml good olive oil
2–3 tbsp. cider vinegar
sea salt
freshly ground pepper

Rinse the split peas in cold water. Put them in a saucepan and cover in water. Add the peeled garlic clove and cook for approx. 35–40 minutes. Make sure that the peas are covered with water throughout.

Take the split peas off the heat and leave for 5 minutes. Drain excess water, but save it for adding to the purée before serving.

Add oil, vinegar, salt and pepper to the split peas and blend with a hand blender until smooth. If the mixture is too thick, you can add some of the water used for cooking the split peas to loosen it a little.

Leave to cool for a little while and add extra salt, pepper and vinegar to taste.

4 people

Rinse the octopus in cold water and then place it in a saucepan. Cover in cold water and add salt as well as coarsely chopped carrot, onion and garlic.

Bring to the boil and then leave the octopus to simmer for approx. 45 minutes. Turn off the heat and leave to settle in the brine for another 30–40 minutes. You want the octopus to be tender, but with a little bite to it. Leave the octopus to cool down in the brine.

Chop the octopus into smaller pieces and marinate in a little garlic, olive oil and freshly chopped rosemary. Place the octopus pieces on a barbecue or on a hot grill pan and cook for 2–3 minutes before turning them over and giving them another 2–3 minutes, which will give them enough caramelization and flavour.

Halve the lemons and place them on the barbecue, cut side down, and cook for 4–5 minutes, which gives them a charred surface.

Add a little lemon juice, freshly ground pepper and nutmeg to the yoghurt.

Take the octopus pieces off the barbecue and sprinkle with sea salt before serving with the chargrilled lemons, yoghurt, chopped almonds and split pea purée.

1 octopus (approx. 1 kg)
1 onion
1 carrot
1 garlic clove
coarse salt
a little finely chopped garlic
some good olive oil
1 rosemary twig
2 unwaxed lemons
100 ml natural yoghurt
sea salt
freshly ground pepper
a little nutmeg
50 g almonds
a little bronze fennel
(alternatively dill, chervil or tarragon)

SEA ROBIN
(GURNARD)

In the UK and elsewhere, this relatively unknown fish has been heavily endorsed by several celebrity chefs, as a sustainable and delicious alternative to the overfished cod and haddock. Not many people know that its Latin name *Triglidae* translates as the more romantic *Sea Robin*. This is also partly due to its appearance: a beaky snout and fins that resemble small wings!

There are three common species of Gurnard – red, yellow and grey, of which the yellow is considered the most tasty. Personally, I like them all, regardless of colour.

Although bony, the flesh is firm and nicely structured, which means you must handle the Gurnard with care, or it'll end up dry and dull. But it's absolutely delicious when fried on its skin side and accompanied by a nice salad.

Gurnard/Sea Robin is at its very best in summer, and to enjoy it, you can grill, marinate and smoke this underappreciated fish.

Fried, marinated
sea robin

4–6 people

Day 1

Make sure the sea robins are fresh – they must smell good, their eyes must be clear and they should be covered in a clear, slippery membrane.

Clean the sea robins; rinse and fillet them (or ask your fish monger to do it for you). Remove any bones and scrape the skin thoroughly.

Fry the fillets on their skin in a little oil on a hot frying pan for approx. 2 minutes, leaving the skin golden and crispy and the flesh still a little raw. Sprinkle with salt and freshly ground pepper.

Remove fillets from the frying pan and place in a deep dish, skin side up.

Peel onions and carrots before slicing the carrots and cutting the onions into thin wedges. Add the vegetables to a saucepan with water, vinegar, fennel seeds, crown dill, peppercorns and sugar. Bring to the boil and pour the pickle over the sea robin fillets as soon as it reaches boiling point. This way the heat from the pickle will complete the cooking of the fillets. Leave the fillets to settle in the fridge for a day.

Day 2

Take the sea robin fillets from the fridge and serve fillets and vegetables as they are, on a piece of rye bread and with a little finely chopped fennel sprinkled on top. You can also heat the fillets in the dish for 8–10 minutes in the oven, at 160°.

The marinated fillets can be served for lunch and dinner, on rye bread or with boiled new potatoes and baked root vegetables. If you can't get hold of sea robin you can also use herrings, mackerel, greater weever, zander, perch, rockfish, etc. In other words, any fish with firm meat that can be fried on its skin side.

4 whole sea robins (300–400 g each) or 8 fillets
2–3 tbsp. rapeseed or maize oil
sea salt
freshly ground pepper
2 red onions
3 carrots
300 ml water
300 ml cider vinegar
10 fennel seeds
2–3 crown dill umbers (this is dill after it has flowered, and is not commonly available however ordinary dill can be used)
10 whole black peppercorns
100 g sugar
½ fennel bulb or a little fennel top

Marinated Sea Robin
with kohlrabi, green strawberries, cream dressing and cress

Marinated sea robin

4–6 people

4 whole sea robins
2 tbsp. soft brown sugar
2 tbs. coarse salt
1 tsp. coriander seeds
1 tsp. fennel seeds
5 juniper berries
1 tsp. dill seeds
freshly ground pepper

Day 1

Make sure the sea robins are fresh – they must smell good, their eyes must be clear and they should be covered in a clear, slippery membrane.

Clean the sea robins, rinse and fillet them (or ask your fishmonger to do it for you). Remove any bones and scrape the skin thoroughly. Then place the fillets in a dish, flesh side up.

Crush the spices in a mortar and then add soft brown sugar and coarse salt.

Spread the spice-mix evenly over the sea robin fillets and then cover the dish with cling film and place in the fridge.

Leave the fillets to marinate for 2 days and turn them over a couple of times during the process. You should leave the fillets for no less than 2 days, but as long as you make sure they are covered and kept in a cold place, you can easily leave them for up to 5–6 days.

Day 3 (or later)

Take the fillets from the dish and slice them finely. Place in another dish or on a plate and serve with a crunchy salad of kohlrabi and green strawberries as well as some good bread as a lunch dish or a starter. You can also serve the marinated sea robin as part of a buffet or as a main course.

SALAD WITH KOHLRABI
AND GREEN STRAWBERRIES

Peel the kohlrabis and slice thinly, using a mandolin or a very sharp knife. Put the kohlrabi in a bowl of cold water – which will help maintain its crunchiness.

Mix the cream, sugar, finely grated lemon zest and lemon juice, olive oil, salt and pepper in a bowl and leave for 15–20 minutes, which will allow the cream to thicken a little.

Wash and hull the strawberries and slice finely.

Add kohlrabi and strawberries to a large bowl and toss with the dressing. Serve on a dish with lots of coarsely chopped cress on top.

2 kohlrabis
50 ml double cream
½ – 1 tbsp. sugar
½ unwaxed lemon
2 tbsp. good olive oil
sea salt
freshly ground pepper
10–15 green, unripe strawberries
1 tray of cress or a bunch of watercress

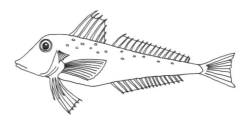

I once had to cook for a large party of 70 people at a restaurant in Copenhagen. They'd ordered sea robin as their main course. This was a little unusual. And when we served the main course, the host came up and said:

"

Excuse me, but there must be some mistake, we've ordered sea robin for our main course, but you've given us fish not fowl!"

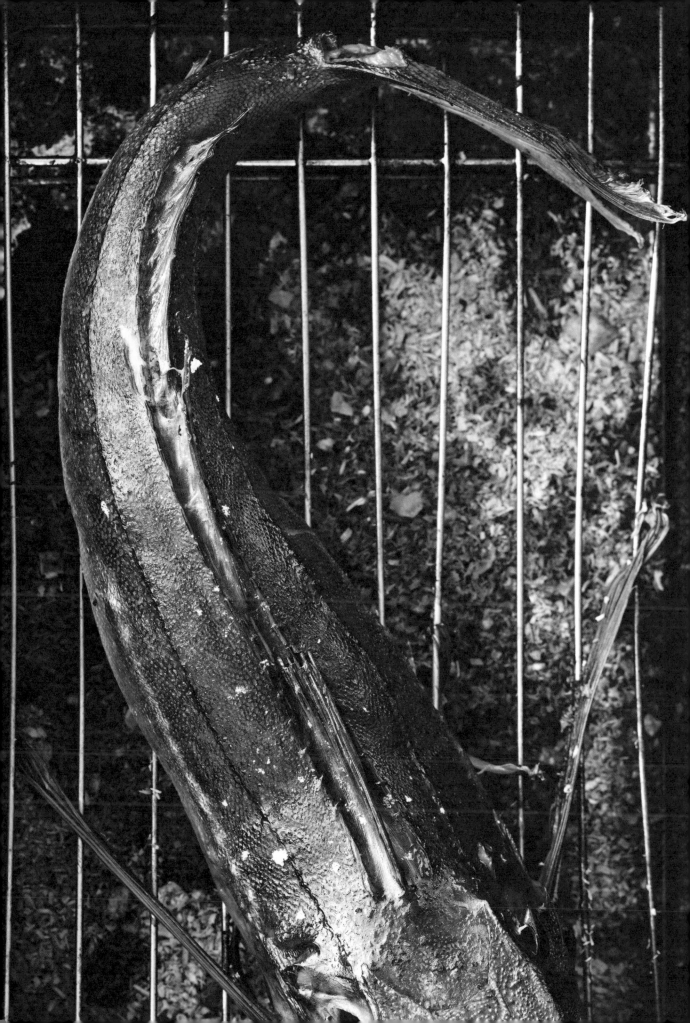

Hot-smoked
sea robin

Make sure the sea robins are fresh – they must smell good, their eyes must be clear and they should be covered in a clear, slippery membrane.

Clean the sea robins thoroughly, removing the guts, and then rinse in cold water before drying with paper tissue. Stuff their cavities with sprigs of rosemary and slices of lemon and sprinkle coarse salt on top. Place in a dish and leave to settle for 1 hour in the fridge.

Place the sea robins on a barbecue inside a small smoking chamber or a bar grill for 10–15 minutes at low heat.

Remove the sea robins from the smoking chamber or bar grill and leave to settle for 10–15 minutes before peeling off the flesh.

Rinse the potatoes and add to a saucepan with enough water to cover them. Bring to the boil and leave to cook for approx. 15 minutes, or until soft. Take potatoes off the heat, drain excess water, and leave to cool slightly.

Mash the potatoes with a whisk and add yoghurt and butter until the purée is soft and smooth. Add salt and freshly ground pepper to taste.

Peel the shallots, top and tail and rinse the radishes before slicing both finely.

Serve potato purée on plates or in a dish, and place pieces of smoked sea robin on top.

Sprinkle radishes and onions on top of the fish, finishing off with a little coarsely chopped lovage and possibly also a little red sorrel.

Serve with good bread as a lunch dish or a starter. This can also be served in small bowls or glasses as tapas or as part of a larger buffet.

2 whole sea robins
4 sprigs of rosemary
½ unwaxed lemon
2 tbsp. coarse salt
600 g small new potatoes
50 ml natural yoghurt
25 g butter
sea salt
freshly ground pepper
2 shallots
8 radishes
½ bunch of lovage
optional: red sorrel as garnish

Grilled sea robin

WITH CAULIFLOWER,
REDCURRANTS AND TARRAGON

4 people

Make sure the sea robin fillets are fresh, and remove any bones.

Place the fillets on a dish and drizzle with a little olive oil before sprinkling salt on top. Leave to settle for 10–15 minutes before frying the fillets on a very hot grill pan.

Remove the outer, green leaves from the cauliflower and throw them away. Chop the cauliflower into smaller pieces before slicing them finely.

Put the cauliflower in a bowl and rinse in cold water. Then place the cauliflower in a sieve and drain.

De-stalk the redcurrants and add to the cauliflower.

Marinate cauliflower and redcurrants in finely grated lemon zest and lemon juice, olive oil, honey, salt, freshly ground pepper and chopped tarragon. Mix well and add extra salt, pepper or lemon to taste.

Grill the sea robin fillets on a very hot grill pan or under an oven grill. Place them on their skin side first for approx. 2 minutes, until their skin is golden and crispy. Be patient and do not turn the fillets over too quickly. Leave them on the grill pan until the skin almost lets go of the pan on its own before turning them over.

Then turn them over and cook for another 10–20 seconds, just finishing them off, ensuring that they do not become overcooked and dry.

Place the grilled fillets on a dish and sprinkle cauliflower, redcurrant and estragon on top.

Serve with good bread as a starter, light lunch dish or as part of a larger meal.

8 sea robin fillets
3–4 tbsp. good olive oil
sea salt
1 cauliflower
100 g redcurrants
1 unwaxed lemon
1 tsp. liquid honey
freshly ground pepper
5 sprigs of tarragon

HERBS

Whether you grow them yourself or buy them at your local greengrocer, fresh herbs are simply fantastic in, around or on top of every kind of food.

Herbs have the power to lift a dish, which only needs that final touch. They smell wonderful and look beautiful, while adding that little extra tanginess, freshness, sweetness or sourness.

Herbs can be used with almost anything and everything: fish, meat, poultry and vegetables – even sweet things such as chocolate, fruits and berries.

In summer, when you'll find copious amounts in your garden or backyard, on your terrace or at your greengrocer, all you have to do is use them, and lots of them.

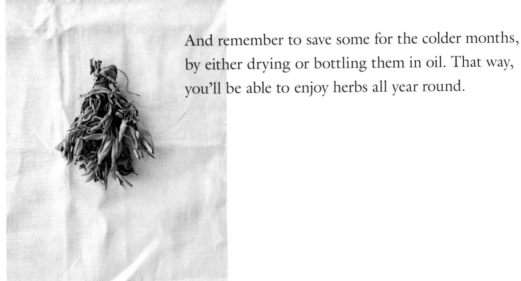

And remember to save some for the colder months, by either drying or bottling them in oil. That way, you'll be able to enjoy herbs all year round.

Thyme in flower

Green gremolata

1 preserving jar of ½ litre

2 unwaxed lemons
1 bunch of flat leaf parsley
1 bunch of mint
50 g sunflower seeds
20 g fennel seeds

Finely grate the lemons and place zest in a bowl.

Rinse the herbs well in cold water and drain.

Chop the herbs quite finely.

Add sunflower seeds while still chopping, mixing them well with the herbs. Then add this mixture to the bowl with lemon zest.

Crush the fennel seeds in a mortar or spice grinder.

Add the crushed fennel seeds to the herb mixture and toss well.

Use to sprinkle on pasta, boiled new potatoes, baked root vegetables, baked or fried fish as well as poultry and other white meats.

It also works really well when sprinkled on cold leftover meat from the previous day. Then all you have to do is finely slice the meat and then sprinkle the herbal mix on top and top it all off with a slight drizzle of olive oil.

You can also keep the gremolata in a glass jar to use another day. It also makes a wonderful homemade gift for your host(ess) if you're visiting friends.

Herb pesto

2 preserving jars of 1 litre

1 bunch of flat leaf parsley
1 bunch of basil
1 unwaxed lemon
1 litre of good olive oil
30 g semi hard cheese,
such as Gouda or Comte
sea salt
freshly ground pepper

Rinse the herbs and drain.

Tear the herbs coarsely, include a little of the stalk, and put in a liquidizer.

Add finely grated lemon zest, olive oil, freshly grated cheese, salt and freshly ground pepper.

Blend everything for approx. 1–2 minutes, until it becomes a smooth and even purée.

Put the pesto in a glass jar or airtight container and keep in the fridge. Unopened it'll keep for 30–45 days. When opened it'll keep for 15–20 days.

Use the pesto as sandwich spread, salad dressing, for tossing baked or raw vegetables in, to drizzle over a juicy steak or some fried or baked fish.

Salt with thyme and sage

1 preserving jar of ½ litre

1 bunch of thyme
1 bunch of sage
200 g coarse salt

Rinse the herbs in cold water and drain. It's important that they are completely dry before mixing them in with the salt.

Roughly tear the herbs and put them in a food processor along with the salt. Mix for 1–2 minutes, until the salt turns green.

You can also chop the herbs finely with a knife and then mix in with the salt. This will give you a slightly coarser version.

Put the salt in a glass jar or an airtight container, which will preserve the scent, flavour and colour of the herbs. The salt will keep for 3–4 weeks, but when freshly made, you get the most potent fresh-herb-experience.

Salt with thyme and sage can be used on meat, poultry and fish before frying – and this will give the finished dish a delicious herbal flavour.

Herbal salt is a brilliant way of using up and preserving herbs when you have a glut of them on your hands.

Dried herbs

herbs
string

Rinse herbs in cold water and drain. They should be completely dry.

Separate your herbs into small, individual bunches and tie the string tightly around the stems.

Hang the bunches upside down in a place where it's airy and dry. In other words, don't leave them in the fridge, but in your kitchen, garden shed or on a balcony.

If you grow lots of herbs in summer, this is a very useful way of preserving them for the cold and dark winter months.

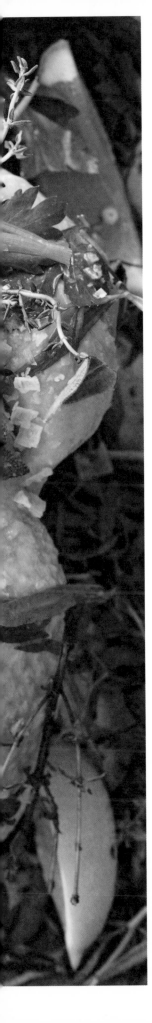

Chicken
stuffed with herbs

Roast chicken

4–6 people

2 large handfuls of herbs
(thyme, sage, rosemary,
tarragon or parsley)
1 free range (if possible) chicken
1 unwaxed lemon
sea salt
freshly ground pepper
50 ml good olive oil

Remove the stalks from half the herbs (but save stalks). Loosen the skin on the chicken breast with your hands, creating a small pocket between skin and breast meat, and stuff the destalked herbs inside.

Place the chicken in an ovenproof dish and stuff some of the herbs and their stalks as well as half a coarsely chopped lemon into the chicken's cavity. Cover the chicken with the remaining herbs, including stalks, as well as the remaining coarsely chopped lemon. Sprinkle with salt and pepper and finally, drizzle some olive oil on top.

Roast the chicken in an oven for 50–60 minutes at 180°, giving it a golden and crispy surface while ensuring that the meat stays moist and soft. If you cook it for too long, the meat will become dry and dull.

Take the chicken out of the oven and leave to sit for 10–15 minutes before carving it into smaller pieces. Serve the chicken with a salad, good bread, boiled or roasted potatoes/root vegetables or whatever else is in season or in your fridge.

BERRIES

In Denmark, as in any temperate climate, we're lucky that our long summers with lots of light, cool nights and warm days bring out the flavour and complexity in our berries, ensuring a perfectly balanced sweetness and acidity.

Summer starts with strawberries, raspberries and redcurrants, followed by gooseberries, blackcurrants and blueberries, ending with full, dark blackberries and elderberries.

In addition to the berries mentioned above, there are lots of other berries that come into their own throughout the year: cowberry, sea buckthorn, rose hip (although botanically they are classed as fruit ...), sloe, chokeberries and so on.

Use these berries in desserts and salads, preserve them as chutney or marmalade or eat them as they are, particularly while you pick them.

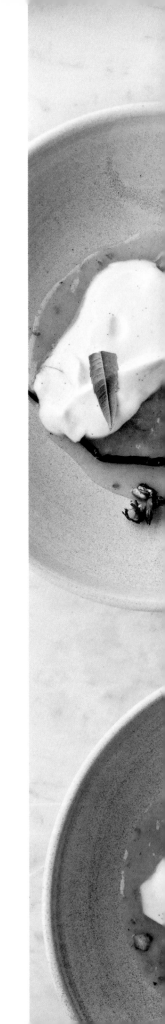

Gooseberry Compote
*with caramelized nuts, seeds
and vanilla yoghurt*

Gooseberry compote

4–6 people

500 g green or red gooseberries
200 g cane sugar
50 ml cider vinegar or lemon juice
a little verbena

Top and tail and rinse the gooseberries.

Put the berries in a flat saucepan with sugar, vinegar and the water that has clung to the berries while being rinsed. Cook until the gooseberries start to mush and collapse. Stir the compote a little to ensure that it is evenly cooked.

Leave to cool and then it's ready to serve.

Serve the compote with vanilla yoghurt and chopped caramelized nuts and seeds, and sprinkle a little fresh verbena on top.

You can also serve this compote with a dollop of good ice cream or as cold gooseberry soup with a little milk on top.

VANILLA YOGHURT

1 vanilla pod
400 ml natural yoghurt
3–4 tbsp. icing sugar
1 unwaxed lemon

Split the vanilla pod and scrape out seeds. Mix yoghurt, icing sugar, vanilla seeds and finely grated lemon zest and lemon juice until smooth.

Leave for 5–10 minutes, allowing the yoghurt to absorb the flavours of both vanilla and lemon. Add a little of everything to taste.

CARAMELIZED NUTS AND SEEDS

Roast the nuts and seeds on a dry frying pan until they turn brown and give off a nutty scent.

Add the honey to the frying pan and toss well with nuts and seeds, ensuring that they are evenly caramelized.

Sprinkle a little salt on top and remove the mixture from the frying pan before it starts to burn.

Leave to cool before coarsely chopping caramelized nuts and seeds.

Keep the caramelized nuts and seeds in an airtight container. You can make double or triple the amount and keep it handy to sprinkle on your morning yoghurt or on a dollop of good ice cream.

100 g mixed nuts
(hazelnuts, almonds, walnuts, pistachio nuts)
100 g mixed seeds
(pumpkin and sunflower seeds)
2 tbsp. liquid honey
sea salt

Baked Blackcurrants
*with verbena, caramel
ice cream and spelt*

Baked blackcurrants

WITH VERBENA, CARAMEL ICE CREAM AND SPELT

CARAMEL ICE CREAM

120 g sugar
400 ml whole milk
200 ml double cream
3–5 grains of salt
7 egg yolks

Add sugar to a saucepan and cook gently until caramelised and golden brown. Then add milk, cream and salt and bring to the boil (you may find the use of salt a bit strange, but you'll find that it cuts the sweetness of the ice cream).

Add the egg yolks to a bowl and carefully whisk in the boiling milk/cream.

Pour the egg & cream mixture back into the saucepan and place it over low heat once more. Carefully heat until it reaches 84–85°, while vigorously stirring – if the cream overheats, it'll turn into scrambled eggs!

Take the saucepan off the heat as soon as the cream starts to thicken, and sieve into a bowl.

Leave the cream to cool for a while and then place in the fridge. Stir from time to time, until it's completely cold.

Add the cream to your ice cream machine and stir until firm and creamy. Then leave the ice cream in your freezer until you need it. The ice cream will maintain a gorgeous creamy texture for 1–2 days.

4–6 people

Wash and de-stalk the blackcurrants. Then put them in an ovenproof dish, lined with baking paper, as this makes it easier to pour the blackcurrants and the juice they give off into a bowl after baking.

Add honey and verbena to the blackcurrants and toss well.

Bake the blackcurrants in the oven for 10–15 minutes at 160°, allowing the currants to break and absorb the honey and verbena flavours.

Take the blackcurrants out of the oven and leave to cool in the dish. Then add to a bowl and place in the fridge, ready for serving.

Serve the baked blackcurrants with caramel ice cream and some spelt flakes sprinkled on top. Add a little fresh verbena on top to taste.

You can also keep the blackcurrant compote in a jar. It's delicious with cheese.

500 g blackcurrants
100 g liquid honey
3–4 verbena sprigs
2 tbsp. spelt flakes

Pickled green strawberries

2 preserving jars of 1 litre

1 kg green, unripe strawberries
1 litre good apple juice
200 ml cider vinegar
15 whole, black peppercorns
15 whole fennel seeds
Sodium benzoate

Rinse strawberries thoroughly in cold water and drain in a colander.

Add apple juice, vinegar and spices to a saucepan and bring to the boil.

Rinse out the preserving jars with sodium benzoate and fill them with green strawberries.

Pour the hot apple juice into the jars – enough to cover the strawberries. Put lid on while the juice is still hot, and leave to cool.

Leave the strawberries to pickle for 2–3 weeks, before eating them. Unopened, they'll keep 5–6 months if kept cool. When opened, they'll keep for 15–20 days.

The pickled strawberries can be used in salads or as a side dish with sausages, ham, cold cuts and poultry.

You can use the strawberry pickle in dressings and marinades or you can reduce it to make a lovely, spicy strawberry syrup.

Rosehip & apple marmalade

1 preserving jar of 1 litre

Put rosehips, water, sugar and finely grated lemon zest and lemon juice in a saucepan.

Split the vanilla pod and scrape out grains. Add both grains and pod to saucepan.

Bring everything to the boil, and leave to cook under a lid for 10–15 minutes, until it thickens into a compote.

Quarter the apples and remove the cores (but save them for later). Cut apples into chunks.

Add apple chunks and cores to the saucepan and leave for another 10 minutes, over low heat, until the apples start to mush, though without losing their shape entirely.

Take the marmalade off the heat and leave to cool for approx. 10 minutes in the saucepan.

Remove the cores and throw them away. There's lots of pectin and lovely bitterness in the apple cores, adding a great almondy flavour to the marmalade, which the pectin also helps to thicken.

Check the taste as well as the marmalade's sweet/ sour balance and add extra lemon juice or sugar if required.

Rinse out the preserving jar with sodium benzoate and pour in the marmalade. Put the marmalade in the fridge, where it'll keep for 1½–2 months if unopened. Once opened, it'll keep for 15–20 days.

Eat the marmalade on a piece of bread, serve with a strong cheese, or over a good quality vanilla ice cream.

400 g rose hips, cleaned
200 ml water
200 g sugar
2 unwaxed lemons
1 vanilla pod
2–3 apples
Sodium benzoate

Blackberry muffins

10–15 muffins

200 g fresh blackberries
2–3 tbsp. liquorice powder
100 g soft butter
200 g cane sugar
3 eggs
100 g wheat flour
50 g white chocolate
50 g coconut flour

Toss the blackberries in liquorice powder and set aside while you assemble the muffin mixture.

Beat the butter and sugar until light and fluffy. Then add one egg at a time. Don't add another egg until the previous one is completely absorbed as this may cause the mixture to separate.

Add the flour, chopped white chocolate and coconut flour. Mix well until the batter is smooth and even. Finally, add the liquorice-coated blackberries.

Pour the batter into muffin-shaped paper or silicone moulds and bake in the oven at 180° for 15 minutes, until they are golden and crispy on the outside and baked in the middle.

The blackberries will collapse a little when baked, but once the muffins have settled, this will merely add some delicious moisture.

Blackberry muffins are best when freshly baked, but you can also put them in a cake tin or airtight container, where they'll keep for a few days. You can in fact also freeze them and simply heat them shortly before serving. They'll be almost as good as when freshly baked.

PUMPKIN

Pumpkins can be used for just about everything: soups, mash, salads, bread, desserts, pickles and jams. As a ground rule, firm pumpkins are better for baking and pickling as they maintain their firmness while being cooked, whereas the softer pumpkins are best in soups and mash.

Pumpkins have a very delicate, yet full and sweet taste, which I think goes really well with herbs such as rosemary, thyme, sage and chervil as well as spices with a touch of aniseed such as fennel seeds, star anise, dill seeds, green anise and root of liquorice.

It's very important to add acidity to a pumpkin dish, i.e. lemon or orange juice, or light, fruity vinegars such as cider, pear or elderflower vinegars, which will enhance the pumpkin's natural fruitiness while breaking down the somewhat heavy and sweet taste that sometimes accompanies pumpkin dishes.

Pickled pumpkin

2 preserving jars

1 Hokkaido or butternut squash
2 tbsp. coarse salt
500 ml cider vinegar
500 ml water
400 g sugar
4 crown dill umbers
4 liquorice roots
4 star anises
10 whole black peppercorns
Sodium benzoate

Day 1

Peel the pumpkin, halve it, and remove seeds. Then slice the pumpkin into slice of approx. 1 cm width (much like pickled cucumber), sprinkle slices with salt and leave to settle for 12 hours in the fridge.

Day 2

Rinse the pumpkin slices in cold water and put them into two preserving jars that have been rinsed out with sodium benzoate.

Add cider vinegar, water and sugar to a saucepan. Divide the crown dill umbers into smaller clusters, break the liquorice roots into smaller bits and add all to the saucepan alongside peppercorns and aniseeds. Bring to the boil.

Pour the boiling pickle juice over the pumpkin slices in the preserving jars and close lids firmly while still hot.

Keep the jars in the fridge or in a dark, cool basement, and leave to settle for approx. 1 week before use. The pickled pumpkins will keep for 6 months when unopened and kept somewhere cool. You can enjoy them with practically everything and anything that goes well with a sour taste.

This recipe is also very useful if you wish to pickle root vegetables such as celeriac, parsley root, Jerusalem artichoke, and parsnip. It even works well with summer vegetables such as cucumber, courgette and green tomatoes.

Pumpkin soup

4–6 people

1 hokkiado or butternut squash
(approx. 800–1000 g)
2 shallots
1 garlic clove
2– 3 tbsp. good olive oil
1 rosemary sprig
1 litre of water or chicken stock
1 unwaxed orange
sea salt
freshly ground pepper
2–3 tbsp. cider vinegar

Garnish
40 fresh or frozen sea buckthorns
2–3 tbsp. sugar
8–12 fresh scallops
2 tbsp. good olive oil
sea salt
freshly ground pepper
20 g almonds
1 bunch of chervil

Halve the pumpkin and remove seeds. Then chop coarsely (don't peel – you can remove the skin when the pumpkin softens as it adds lovely flavour and colour to the soup).

Peel and chop onions and garlic.

Sautée the pumpkin pieces gently in oil with onions, garlic and rosemary. Add water or stock and finely grated zest of orange, and leave to boil for 15–20 minutes, until the pumpkin is soft.

Take out the sprig of rosemary and blend the soup in a liquidizer until smooth and creamy. Add salt, pepper and vinegar to taste, making sure you hit the right balance. The sweet-tasting pumpkin needs plenty of spices, or the soup will lack zest.

Add sea buckthorn and sugar to a small saucepan and bring to the boil, and quickly remove the saucepan from the heat. You need to heat the sea buckthorn a little for it to absorb the sugar, which releases its lovely tropical fruity flavours (mango, passion fruit and papaya).

Fry the scallops in some oil on a hot frying pan for approx. 30 seconds each side, which will give them a good crust, while leaving their middle soft and succulent. Add salt and freshly ground pepper to taste.

Serve the pumpkin soup in heated bowls or deep plates with a couple of scallops in each. Sprinkle sea buckthorn, chopped almonds and chervil on top. Serve the soup as a starter or a lunch dish.

Baked pumpkin salad

WITH SALTED AND SMOKED COMMON DAB, LINGONBERRIES, JERUSALEM ARTICHOKE AND SHALLOTS

4 people

Peel the pumpkin and remove seeds. Chop coarsely (possibly in wedges) and place on a baking sheet covered with baking paper. Cover the pieces with vinegar, oil, honey, salt and pepper.

Bake the pumpkin pieces in the oven for 7–8 minutes at 180°, until soft but with a little bite.

Take them out of oven and leave to cool.

Toss the lingonberries in cane sugar and leave to settle on the kitchen table for 10 minutes.

Wash the Jerusalem artichokes thoroughly; use a sponge to make sure you remove all earth. Then slice thinly, using a mandolin or a very sharp knife.

Toss the baked pumpkin pieces with the lingonberries, Jerusalem artichokes and chopped chervil. Add extra salt and pepper to taste.

Peel the shallot and slice finely.

Fillet the common dab and peel the skin off – you can also get your fishmonger to do this. Make sure there are no bones left before cutting the fillets into small squares. Fry on a hot frying pan, in a little olive oil, until crisp.

Serve the pumpkin on a dish, and sprinkle with shallot and fried fish squares.

Serve as a lunch dish on its own or as part of a larger menu. The salad also works well as a side dish with fish.

If you can't get your hands on salted and smoked common dab or flounder, you can use bacon instead.

1 large Hokkaido or butternut squash
4 tbsp. vinegar cider
4 tbsp. good olive oil
2 tbsp. liquid honey
sea salt
freshly ground pepper
100 ml fresh or frozen lingonberries (cranberries are a good substitute also)
1 tbsp. cane sugar
200 g Jerusalem artichokes
1 bunch of chervil
1 large shallot
1 whole salted and smoked common dab (200–300 g) (flounder is good substitute)

Sweet Pumpkin Purée

*with liquorice ice cream and a fresh salad
with pumpkin, apple and lemon*

Sweet pumpkin purée

4–6 people

1 Hokkaido or butternut squash (save one pumpkin wedge for the salad)
1 liquorice root
25 g butter
2–3 tbsp. liquid honey
1 unwaxed lemon

Halve the pumpkin and remove seeds – leave the peel on as it will soften during cooking and add extra colour and taste to the purée. Cut the pumpkin into large pieces.

Add pumpkin pieces and liquorice root to a saucepan and cover with water. Bring to the boil and cook for approx. 20 minutes, until soft, and then drain in a colander.

Put the soft pumpkin pieces in a liquidizer with butter and honey and blend until completely smooth.

Add finely grated lemon zest and lemon juice to taste and leave to cool and settle for 15–20 minutes. You can add extra lemon and honey to taste once it's cooled down.

Serve with a scoop of liquorice ice cream and fresh pumpkin & apple salad (see below). Sprinkle the herbs on top.

LIQUORICE ICE CREAM

Put sugar, milk, cream, liquorice powder and salt
in a saucepan and bring to the boil (you may find
the use of salt a bit strange, but you'll find it cuts
through the sweetness of the ice cream and enhances
the taste of liquorice).

Add the egg yolks to a bowl and carefully whisk in
the boiling milky cream.

Pour the mixture back into the saucepan and leave
on the hob, and carefully heat until it reaches
80–84° while whisking vigorously.

Take the saucepan off the heat once the cream starts
to thicken – if the cream becomes too hot, it'll
coagulate and separate!

Leave the cream to sit for 10–15 minutes, and then
sieve it back into the bowl and place in the fridge.
Stir occasionally until completely cold.

Add the cream to an ice cream maker and stir until
firm and creamy. Then place in the freezer until you
need it. The ice cream will maintain its lovely and
creamy texture for 1–2 days.

150 g sugar
400 ml whole milk
200 ml double cream
3–5 tbsp. liquorice powder
3–5 grains of salt
7 egg yolks

SALAD WITH PUMPKIN AND APPLE

1 apple
1 wedge of pumpkin (left over
from the purée)
1 tsp. liquid honey
a little lemon juice
some fresh wood sorrel, lemon balm
or verbena

Quarter the apple and remove core.

Slice both apple and pumpkin finely,
using a mandoline, and place in a bowl.

Marinate apple and pumpkin quickly
in lemon juice and honey, retaining a
little bite.

BRUSSELS SPROUTS

In my opinion, Brussels sprouts are a highly underrated and often overlooked vegetable. Their delicate texture, crunchiness and mild bitterness renders them unlike most other vegetables. And on top of that Brussels sprouts – well, any kind of cabbage really – makes for healthy and inexpensive eating.

Brussels sprouts are well suited to a temperate climate of cool summers and cold winters. Frost takes the edge off the sprouts' sharp taste and you can actually leave them outside all through winter. Sprouts will easily keep for up to two weeks in the fridge. And if you have the facilities, you can also leave them outside.

As a general rule, you should prepare Brussels sprouts only minimally. The worst you can possibly do is overcook them. If you give them more than 5–6 minutes, they'll taste bland and bitter and their vivid, variegated green colour will turn to a camouflage sludge.

Personally, I love raw Brussels sprouts. Either finely sliced or plucked, which will allow you to marinate the beautiful whole leaves. Roasted Brussels sprouts are also one of my favourites. And they make a wonderful purée, but again, it's important that they're not overcooked, i.e. boil them just up until they start to turn soft.

Brussels sprouts purée

4 people

1 kg Brussels sprouts
a little coarse salt
25 g butter
50 ml good olive oil
1 unwaxed lemon
sea salt
freshly ground pepper
2 shallots
3 tbsp. cider vinegar
1 tsp. liquid honey
2 pears
some chervil
25 g walnuts

Cut the stems off the Brussels sprouts. Remove the outer leaves and throw away the ugly ones but keep the nicer looking ones for the salad. Quarter the remaining core of Brussels sprouts and rinse in cold water.

Bring a saucepan with lightly salted water to the boil and add the Brussels sprouts. Cook for a couple of minutes – make sure they turn soft, but don't leave them for too long, because that may result in a slightly 'farty' taste and smell.

Add the Brussels sprouts and 50–100 ml of the boiling water to a food processor or liquidizer and blend with butter, half the olive oil and finely grated lemon zest until smooth. Add salt and pepper to taste.

Peel the shallots and slice in rings with a width of approx. ½ – 1 cm. Add to a bowl and marinate in cider vinegar and honey. Toss well, and leave for 10–15 minutes. This will ensure that the onions stay crunchy while losing some of their strong onion taste.

Quarter the pears and remove core. Cut into fine wedges.

Toss the raw Brussels sprouts leaves with the pear wedges, chopped chervil and walnuts, the marinated shallots and the accompanying juice. Toss well and add salt and pepper as well as the last bit of olive oil to taste.

Serve the purée in a dish with the salad on top.

Serve as a lunch dish or as a side order with fish, poultry or light meat.

Roasted
Brussels sprouts

WITH CHILLI, LIME,
PARSLEY AND COD ROE

Cut the stems off the Brussels sprouts. Remove the tough, outer leaves and throw them away. Quarter the remaining core of Brussels sprouts and rinse well in cold water. Leave them in a colander to drain.

Boil the cod roe (see recipe below).

Roast the Brussels sprouts in some olive oil on a hot frying pan for approx. 1–2 minutes, allowing them to turn slightly golden and even become a little charred on the outside.

Add coarsely chopped parsley, finely chopped chilli, honey and freshly grated lime zest and juice and toss well in the pan.

Add salt and pepper to taste and take the frying pan off the heat, which ensures that the Brussels sprouts are not overcooked, and have maintained their freshness and crunchiness, with a slightly charred and caramelized flavour.

Serve the warm Brussels sprouts with the boiled cod roe, which can be served either warm or cold. Serve this dish for lunch with good bread. You can also serve it as a starter or part of a larger buffet.

You can even serve the roasted Brussels sprouts as a side dish with fish, fishcakes or poultry. If you make a big batch, you can also mix in some noodles, instantly creating a stunning vegetarian dish.

300 g Brussels sprouts
2–3 tbsp. good olive oil
1 bunch of flat leaf parsley
½ fresh red chilli
1 tsp. liquid honey
2 unwaxed limes
sea salt
freshly ground pepper
400 g freshly cooked cod roe

BOILED COD ROE

Place the cod roe in a saucepan, cover with cold water and the rest of the ingredients. Carefully bring to the boil, skimming any froth off the top, once it starts to boil.

Cook over low heat for 4–6 minutes, and then turn off the heat, but leave the roe to steep in its broth until cool.

You can serve the cod roe cold or warm, as it is, or tossed in flour and fried in butter.

1 kg fresh cod roe
10 whole black peppercorns
3 bay leaves
2 tbsp. white wine vinegar
2 tbsp. coarse salt

Brussels sprouts salad

4 people

100 whole rye kernels
3–4 tbsp. cider vinegar
50 ml good olive oil
400 g Brussels sprouts
3 carrots
2 apples
(preferably with some acidity and bite)
1 tsp. liquid honey
sea salt
freshly ground pepper
½ bunch of fresh mint
1 handful red wood sorrel

Put the rye kernels into a colander and rinse in cold water. Drain, tip into a saucepan and add fresh water until covered.

Bring to the boil and simmer for approx. 50 minutes at low heat – keep an eye on them to ensure there's always enough water. You don't want the kernels to boil dry.

You can also cook the kernels the day before, and keep them in the fridge until you need them.

Take the kernels off the heat and add to a bowl. Marinate in a little salt, 1 tbsp. vinegar and 1 tbsp. olive oil, allowing them to absorb the flavours while cooling.

Cut the stems off the Brussels sprouts. Remove the tough, outer leaves and throw them away.

Peel the carrots, quarter the apples and remove the core.

Finely slice the Brussels sprouts, carrots and apples and add to a bowl.

Toss with the now cooled kernels, the rest of the olive oil, vinegar, honey, salt and freshly ground pepper.

Pluck and chop the mint leaves and mix in with the salad. Finally, sprinkle a little sorrel on top.

Serve as a salad on its own or as a side dish with poultry, light meat or fish.

Brussels sprouts and plaice

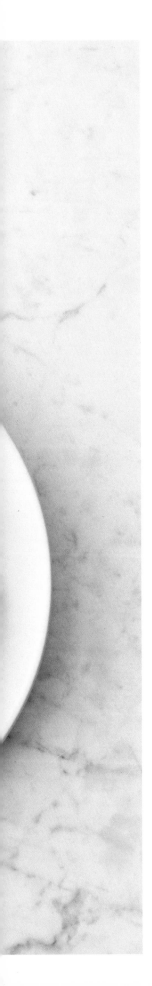

4 people

4 skinned plaice	Rinse the plaice in cold water and check that they are properly cleaned.
a little wheat flour	
sea salt	
freshly ground pepper	Halve each plaice, toss in some flour and sprinkle with salt and pepper.
1 shallot	
25 g butter for frying	
100 ml white wine	Peel the shallot and slice coarsely. Add to a saucepan with 10 g butter.
½ litre chicken stock	
200 g Brussels sprouts	
4 tomatoes	Sautée the sliced shallots for 1–2 minutes, until soft and transparent.
50 g almonds	
1 bunch of tarragon	
30 g cold butter for the sauce	Add white wine and chicken stock and bring to the boil. Leave to simmer until reduced by half. Sieve into another saucepan and set aside for later.
2–3 tbsp. good olive oil	

Cut off the stems and pluck the tough outer leaves off each sprout and rinse in cold water.

Quarter the tomatoes and remove the seeds and core, then dice finely.

Chop almonds and tarragon coarsely.

Re-heat the chicken stock and carefully whisk in small nobs of butter until it thickens. Once the butter is added, do not bring to the boil, as the sauce will separate.

Heat a frying pan and fry the plaice in oil and butter for approx. 2–3 minutes on each side, giving them a golden and crispy coating.

Remove the plaice from the frying pan and place on a plate or dish.

Add Brussels sprouts, tomatoes, almonds and tarragon to the sauce and heat gently.

Pour the sauce over the plaice and serve immediately, possibly with new potatoes, a nice salad, some boiled fresh vegetables or just with good bread.

PICNIC

N 56° 3.513'
E 12° 4.411'

In spring the woods are crammed with wild herbs, followed by abundant berries, after which it's time for picking mushrooms.

Read about which mushrooms you should pick, and make sure you only pick those you are certain aren't poisonous. Chanterelles and boletuses are some of the best you can find, and also some of the easiest to recognize.

Bring a blanket and some simple dishes and spend most of the day in the woods, walking, eating and hunting for herbs, berries or mushrooms. Finish the day off with a cup of coffee and something sweet.

Rye bread sandwich

4 people

1 red onion
a little sugar
sea salt
2 tbsp. cider vinegar
2 avocados
8 slices of nice rye bread
60 g good quality goat's cheese
10–15 basil leaves
freshly ground pepper

Peel the red onion and halve. Then slice finely.

Add onion slices to a bowl and sprinkle with a little salt and sugar before dripping some vinegar on top. Then toss and leave to marinate on the kitchen table for 30 minutes.

Halve the avocados. Remove the stone and peel before slicing. Spread the avocado on four slices of rye bread.

Also spread the goat's cheese, basil leaves and marinated red onion slices, sprinkle with a little salt and pepper and put the remaining four slices of rye bread on top.

Wrap the sandwiches in paper and bring on your picnic.

Soup of Parsley Root

with browned butter, preserved lemon and
marinated chanterelles

Soup of parsley root

4 people

500 g parsley roots
2 shallots
30 g butter
1 slice of preserved lemon
1 litre water
300 ml whole milk
sea salt
freshly ground pepper

Peel parsley roots and shallots and chop coarsely.

Add butter to a saucepan and place on a heated hob, allowing the butter to sizzle before browning, which gives off a nutty smell.

Add parsley roots, onions and coarsely chopped preserved lemon to the saucepan and sautée for 1–2 minutes, until they get a little colour (if you haven't preserved the lemon, you can use a little freshly grated lemon zest instead).

Add water and bring to the boil. Leave cooking at low heat for 10–15 minutes, until the parsley roots turn soft.

Add milk and salt and pepper to taste, and leave to cook for another 5 minutes.

Take the saucepan off the heat and blend the soup using a liquidizer or a hand blender until the soup is smooth and even.

Pour the soup back into the saucepan and heat gently. You can add extra salt, pepper and salted lemon to taste.

Pour the soup into an airtight thermos and bring on your picnic.

Serve the soup in paper cups with some marinated chanterelles (see previous page) at the bottom. Serving hot soup for lunch is wonderful when you're out for a walk in the woods, or if you're hunting for mushrooms.

MARINATED CHANTERELLES

300 g chanterelles
1 garlic clove
10 whole black peppercorns
sea salt
2 thyme sprigs
2 tbsp. cider vinegar
200 ml good olive oil

Thoroughly clean the chanterelles and cut them into smaller pieces if necessary.

Add garlic, peppercorns, a little salt, thyme, vinegar and olive oil to a saucepan and heat until it reaches 60–70°.

Put the chanterelles in a preserving jar and pour the hot oil on top.

Close the lid and leave in room temperature for 7–14 days, before using them.

You can leave the chanterelles for 6–8 months, as long as they are covered in oil. You can also store them in a cool place, but then the oil will coagulate.

You can make large batches of marinated chanterelles and use them throughout winter in soups and salads, as a sandwich filling and with cold cuts. You can use the oil for marinades and dressings or to whip up a lovely chanterelle mayo.

PRESERVED LEMONS
1 large preserving jar

Rinse the lemons and quarter 5 of the lemons from the top almost all the way down to the bottom. They should not separate completely.

Put salt inside the lemons and place them in a large preserving jar, pressing them closely together. Add the remaining salt and squeeze the juice from the remaining lemon into the jar before closing the lid. Place the salted lemons somewhere dark and cool for at least 1 month before using them.

You can use these lemons as a spice and flavour enhancer in soups and stews as well as with roast poultry and in salads. Use the whole lemon and cut it into smaller pieces, but make sure to remove the bitter pips first. You can also blend a little of the fruit meat and use it in dressings. You cannot, however, re-use the salt, which will have turned to brine.

6 unwaxed lemons
300–400 ml coarse sea salt

Chanterelles and boletuses

Mushroom tapenade

TOASTED BREAD

¼ day-old wheat loaf
2–3 tbsp. good olive oil
sea salt

Slice the bread thinly and place on baking paper on a baking sheet.

Drizzle olive oil on top and sprinkle with sea salt.

Place the baking sheet in the oven and bake for 7–8 minutes at 180°, until crispy and golden.

4 people

Thoroughly clean the mushrooms and cut into smaller pieces.

Add oil, the whole garlic clove, thyme and mushrooms to a saucepan and leave to sautée for a couple of minutes. Then put a lid on the saucepan and leave the mushrooms to fry/steam at low heat for approx. 10 minutes, until they collapse.

Remove the saucepan from the heat and leave the mushrooms to settle for 5 minutes before blending them.

Put mushrooms and accompanying liquid into a liquidizer, but remove thyme sprigs and garlic clove before blending to a smooth and even paste. Add lemon juice, salt and freshly ground pepper to taste.

Put the warm mushroom tapenade in a preserving jar and close the lid. This makes it easy to bring on a picnic, and of course, it's also a useful way to keep it in your fridge at home.

Serve the mushroom tapenade with toasted bread as a little appetizer at your picnic. You can also serve it on your terrace with a glass of cold white wine to kick off a barbecue.

500 g wild mushrooms,
preferably chanterelles and boletuses
3 tbsp. good olive oil
1 garlic clove
5 thyme sprigs
½ lemon
sea salt
freshly ground pepper

Crunchy cookies

Approx. 50 cookies

250 g soft butter
300 g sugar
1 tsp. fine sea salt
2 eggs
340 g wheat flour
2 tsp. liquorice powder
1 tsp. baking soda
1 tsp. boiling water
200 g white chocolate

Whisk butter, sugar and salt using an electric whisk or a food mixer until thoroughly combined. Add the eggs, one at a time, and mix well. Then add wheat flour and liquorice powder little by little, and mix everything well.

Dissolve the baking soda in boiling water and mix in with the dough. Coarsely chop the chocolate and mix into dough as well. Divide the dough into 2–3 rolls of approx. 2–3 cm in width, and wrap the 'sausages' in baking paper. Then leave in the fridge for at least 2 hours, but overnight is even better.

Put baking paper on two baking sheets. Cut the dough-sausages into slices of 2–3 mm in width and place the cookies on the baking sheet. Make sure there's plenty of space between them.

Bake the cookies in the oven for 7–10 minutes at 175°, until golden around the edges. Then take them out of the oven and leave to cool on a wire rack (on baking paper).

You can easily make the cookies a couple of days before you need them, as long as you keep them in an airtight tin. They'll keep their crunchiness for 10–14 days. Bring cookies and primus stove on your picnic and make a good, strong cup of coffee, instant or cowboy-fashion, which you can serve with the cookies.

OFFAL

Offal is a healthy, cheap and delicious food, yet is undervalued and underappreciated by most. The problem is too many people have been served liver that was as tough as leather, or kidneys that were not properly de-veined as well as tongue or heart that should have been cooked to a soft and melting consistency but were, in fact, quite the opposite.

If you treat offal with the respect it deserves and prepare it properly, then you'll experience something completely different. Tasting succulent liver with a pink middle as well as tender and aromatic kidneys will obliterate any previous antipathy.

When you buy offal, it's important to go for quality and freshness. Whichever parts you buy must smell fresh. Liver, kidneys and hearts must have a rich red colour, no spots or broken membranes. Sweetbreads must be light in colour and their membranes transparent and shiny. Tongue must also be light in colour with an intact and slightly nobbly surface.

Liver, kidneys, heart, tongue and sweetbread – I love them all, and I will happily tuck into any dish using these ingredients. My favourite is hearts in cream sauce, just like my grandmother used to make it, and my mother after her: pigs' or calves' hearts stuffed with apples, prunes and lots of chopped parsley, bathed in a sea of delicious cream sauce. I'm afraid I rarely get to indulge, as I'm the only member of my own family who happens to count this as an all time great. (It should be said that offal is an acquired taste, not normally enjoyed by any small person under the age of 12).

Grilled lamb's heart

WITH A CHERRY VINAIGRETTE, KOHLRABI AND RADICCHIO

100 g cherries, possibly without stones
50 ml cherry vinegar
50 ml good rapeseed oil
2 tbsp. liquid honey
sea salt
freshly ground pepper
2 hearts of lamb
1 radicchio
1 kohlrabi
3–4 tbsp. good olive oil
5 thyme sprigs
1 tray of cress

Place the cherries in an ovenproof dish and drizzle with vinegar, rapeseed oil, honey, salt and pepper.

Place dish in the oven and bake for 7–8 minutes at 180°, until they turn soft, yet maintain their shape.

Take the cherries out of the oven and leave to cool for 45–60 minutes. You can pour the cherry vinaigrette into a preserving jar and keep in the fridge for use some other time.

Halve the lamb's hearts and get rid of any remaining blood vessels or membranes. Then add to a bowl with cold water and leave to soak for 30–60 minutes.

Cut the radicchio into smaller pieces and rinse in cold water before leaving it in a colander to drain.

Peel the kohlrabi and slice finely using a mandolin or a peeler. Then add to a bowl with cold water and leave for 10–15 minutes – this increases the crispiness of the kohlrabi.

Toss the lamb's hearts in some olive oil and chopped thyme and grill on a hot grill pan for approx. 30 seconds on each side, which will give them a nice crust while keeping them rosy and succulent in the middle. Remove the hearts from the grill pan and add salt and freshly ground pepper to taste.

Leave the lamb's hearts to settle for 2–3 minutes, before slicing them finely.

Toss radicchio and kohlrabi with the cherry vinaigrette and serve the salad on a dish with slices of lamb's heart and cress on top.

Serve as a starter or as part of a larger buffet and preferably with good bread.

Fried calf's liver

4 people

800 g – 1 kg fresh calf's liver
a little wheat flour
sea salt
freshly ground pepper
2 red onions
3–4 tbsp. cider vinegar
1 tsp. liquid honey
1 bunch of flat leaf parsley
15–20 fennel seeds
50 g freshly grated North Sea
cheese (use Gouda or Comte
as substitutes)
2–3 tbsp. good olive oil

Make sure that the liver is fresh – it should be deep red and smell fresh.

Remove any remaining membranes and blood vessels and cut into fine slices of approx. 2 cm in width.

Turn the slices over in some flour, salt and pepper and leave on a plate before placing in the fridge.

Peel and halve the onions. Then slice them finely and add to a bowl. Toss with vinegar, honey, salt and pepper. Leave the onions to marinate on the kitchen table for 1–2 hours.

Rinse the parsley, drain and chop. Mix the chopped parsley with the lightly crushed fennel seeds, grated cheese and add salt and pepper to taste.

Heat a frying pan and fry the liver slices in olive oil for 1–2 minutes on each side, depending on how rosy you want them in the middle.

Take the frying pan off the heat. Sprinkle with red onions, parsley, cheese and fennel seeds, and serve immediately. Liver is quite simply best when served fresh off the frying pan, its centre rosy and succulent.

Fried calf's sweetbread

4 people

Place the sweetbread in a saucepan and cover with cold water, salt, bay leaves, peppercorns and vinegar. Bring to the boil and skim off froth when boiling. Lower the heat once the sweetbread reaches boiling point, then simmer for 5 minutes over low heat.

Take the sweetbread off the heat and leave to cool in the brine. Once it's cold, remove any remaining membranes and fat.

Cut the sweetbread into smaller pieces and add to a hot frying pan. Fry in oil for 2–3 minutes on each side, leaving them crispy and with a beautiful, golden crust. Be careful you don't fry too many pieces at the same time, as they may start boiling instead, and it's important that they get a crispy and golden crust. You're better off just frying a few pieces of sweetbread at a time.

Add salt and pepper to taste and serve on top of turnips, redcurrants and wood sorrel.

600 g fresh calf's sweetbread
(order in advance from your butcher)
coarse salt
3 bay leaves
10 whole black peppercorns
1 tbsp. cider vinegar
good olive oil
sea salt
freshly ground pepper

TURNIPS WITH REDCURRANT AND WOOD SORREL

Peel the turnips and cut into large pieces. Then add to boiling, lightly salted water and cook for 1–2 minutes, until they turn soft.

Drain the turnips and marinate in vinegar, olive oil, mustard, honey, salt and pepper while still hot. It's important that the turnips are marinated while still hot as they absorb the flavours better that way, and it's important that the sweet and sour marinade balances the turnips' natural bitterness.

Rinse the wood sorrel and dry lightly in a tea towel. Then chop coarsely and add to the turnips and redcurrants. Toss well and add extra salt and pepper to taste.

You can also serve the turnips as a 'salad' on its own or as a side dish with fried fish or poultry.

12 turnips
coarse salt
50 ml cider vinegar
1 tbsp. good olive oil
1 tbsp. Dijon mustard
1 tsp. liquid honey
sea salt
freshly ground pepper
1 handful of red wood sorrel
(alternatively, you can use lemon
balm, verbena or parsley)
100 g fresh and de-stalked
redcurrants

Calf's kidney

4 people

200 g fresh calf's kidney
50 ml soy sauce
50 ml balsamic or dark, fruity vinegar
1 tbsp. liquid honey
4–5 tbsp. good olive oil
1 large broccoli
sea salt
freshly ground pepper
300 g sesame seeds
½ bunch of bronze fennel
(alternatively chervil or tarragon)

Make sure the kidney is fresh – it should be a deep red and smell fresh. Cut the kidney into smaller pieces and remove the larger sinews. Add the kidney pieces to a bowl and leave to soak in cold water with a dash of vinegar for 30–40 minutes. Then remove them from the water and dry thoroughly.

Add soy sauce, balsamic vinegar and honey to a saucepan and bring to the boil, and leave it to cook until reduced into half.

Take the saucepan off the heat and whisk in half the olive oil, which will turn it into a thick and smooth soy dressing.

Add the dressing to a bowl and leave to cool.

Divide the broccoli into large bouquets and peel the stalk, which you'll also use. The stalk has a nice crunchiness to it and a mild nutty taste mixed with a little sharpness.

Blanch the broccoli in lightly salted water for ½ – 1 minute and put in cold water immediately after, as this will ensure that the broccoli keeps both crunchiness and colour.

Heat a frying pan and fry the kidney pieces in a little olive oil over strong heat for approx. 1 minute on each side, giving them a nice crust while maintaining a rosy and succulent centre. Add salt and freshly ground pepper to taste.

Remove the kidney pieces from the frying pan and leave to settle for 1–2 minutes, before slicing them thinly.

Serve the broccoli on a plate or dish, with slices of kidney and soy dressing on top. Finally, sprinkle sesame seeds and bronze fennel on top.

Serve the kidneys for lunch or as a starter. You can also make this dish with lamb's kidneys, calf's liver or even fried chicken or fish.

Boiled lamb's tongue

1 carrot
1 garlic clove
1 onion
4 lamb's tongues
3 bay leaves
coarse salt
10 whole black peppercorns
1 beetroot
50 ml cherry vinegar
50 ml good olive oil
1 tsp. liquid honey
sea salt
freshly ground pepper
200 g de-stalked kale
20 g freshly ground horseradish

Peel the carrot, garlic and onion and cut into large chunks.

Put the lamb's tongues in a saucepan along with water, carrot, garlic, onion, bay leaves, salt and whole peppercorns. Bring to the boil and leave to simmer for approx. 45 minutes, skimming off the froth to avoid impurities.

Take the saucepan off the heat and leave the tongues to cool down in the brine for 15 minutes.

Then remove the tongues and pull their membranes off using a small knife. Place the tongues back in the brine and leave to cool off completely.

Peel the beetroot and cut into paper-thin slices using a mandolin. Add the beetroot slices to a bowl.

Toss the beetroot with vinegar, olive oil, honey salt and pepper.

Rinse the kale well in a bowl with cold water, and leave to drain in a colander.

Tear the kale into small pieces and add to the sliced beetroot before leaving to marinate. Add finely grated horseradish to taste.

Split the lamb's tongues in half and serve with the beetroot-kale salad on top. Drizzle some of the marinade over everything.

Serve the tongues as a starter, with Sunday lunch or as part of a larger menu with lots of smaller dishes.

Lamb's tongue is a rarely used ingredient, but it's delicious. It's soft, tender and lean – and it doesn't taste of lamb at all.

PORK

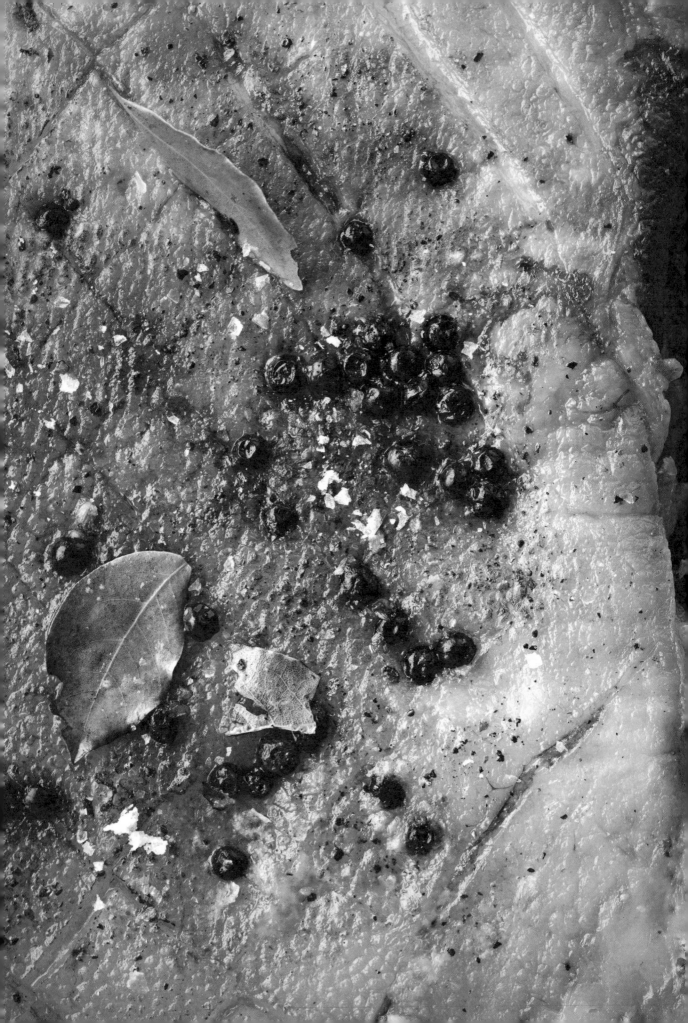

Pigs that have led happy lives produce the finest meat. Pork is extremely popular in Denmark, as it is worldwide, and much of the pork we consume here is of a very high quality. Miraculously, there' s a growing, worldwide demand for standards to be raised even higher, as consumers ask for free range, organic, and rare breeds. People also like to know that the pigs have preferably been allowed to roam free, having a lovely time snuffling the ground and eating whatever they find.

You can use practically every part of a pig – an old Danish proverb states that the only thing you can't eat is the pig's squeal. So grill, braise, roast, fry, boil, chop and eat pork.

The colour of the meat can vary quite a bit, depending on the breed and age of the pig. But a good rule of thumb is to go for the pink meat lined with white fat – of which there shouldn't be too much. If it comes with scratching (skin), it must be thin, firm and intact.

Everyone in my family is fond of pork, but we prefer to eat less in favour of spending a little more money to buy the best quality we can get our hands on.

Slow roasted breast of pork

Gently score the fat on the breast of pork and place the meat in an ovenproof dish. Pour the apple juice and beer over the meat and rub the surface with sea salt, whole juniper berries, bay leaves and peppercorns.

Place the dish in the oven to roast for 2–2½ hours at 140°. Keep basting the meat with the beer and apple juices at least a couple of times during roasting.

Take the dish out of the oven and leave the meat to settle for 10–15 minutes before slicing. The meat should be golden and caramelized on the outside and tender and succulent in the middle. It should practically fall apart when cut.

Serve slices of roasted breast of pork with a little of the pan juices and the warm, fried kale.

Serve as a hearty lunch dish with bread or as a main course with potatoes or baked root vegetables.

1–1½ kg breast of pork with bones but without skin
200 ml good apple juice
200 ml beer, preferably dark
sea salt
15 whole juniper berries
10 bay leaves
10 whole black peppercorns

STIR-FRIED PALM KALE

Mix mustard, vinegar, honey and 4 tbsp. olive oil with salt and freshly ground pepper until you have a good, thick dressing.

Peel the red onions, then halve and slice thinly.

Toss the red onions with the dressing and leave to marinate for 5–10 minutes, allowing the onions to soften.

Pluck the kale from its stalk and divide into smaller bits. Put the kale in a bowl and rinse well with cold water.

Then place the kale in a colander and leave to drain.

Fry the kale on a hot frying pan in a little olive oil for approx. 30 seconds at a very high temperature, while tossing the kale. You just want the kale to collapse and get a slightly charred surface, but you mustn't fry it for too long, as you want the kale to stay crunchy and beautifully green.

2 tbsp. coarse mustard
3–4 tbsp. cider vinegar
1 tbsp. honey
5 tbsp. good olive oil
sea salt
freshly ground pepper
2 red onions
approx. 500 g de-stalked palm kale (1 stalk)

Remove the kale from the frying pan and toss with sliced red onions and dressing.

Serve the fried kale with the slow roasted breast of pork or with fried pork sausage, braised pork jowls or boiled knuckle of pork. It also works really well with grilled chicken or fish.

If you can't find palm kale, use curly kale or black kale instead.

Braised cheeks of pork

Start by removing the membrane from the pork cheeks, if your butcher hasn't already done it. To do this, place the cheeks on the chopping board, membrane downward and completely flat against the board. Take a long, sharp knife and make a small incision in the meat, right next to the membrane. Grab hold of the membrane and allow the knife to cut along the membrane, down towards the board, removing the membrane with one clean cut.

Brown the cheeks in a bit of olive oil in a saucepan, until they are coloured on all sides. Remove from the pan and set aside while you deal with the vegetables.

Peel the carrots, onions and garlic and cut into large chunks. Add vegetables to the saucepan and brown before adding back the cheeks, thyme, beer, apple juice, vinegar, salt and pepper. Reduce the liquid to half, then add the stock and slowly bring to the boil. Skim the froth to get rid of impurities. Then put a lid on top and place the cheeks in the oven and leave to braise for 1½ – 2 hours at 150°.

Remove saucepan from oven and sieve the broth into another saucepan – throw the vegetables away and put the cheeks back into the empty saucepan. In the full saucepan, bring the stock to the boil and reduce to half, giving it a nice and sticky consistency as well as a shiny surface. Add butter, salt and cider vinegar to taste. Once the stock is perfectly flavoured, add pork cheeks and heat together.

Top and tail the green beans and blanch in lightly salted water, ready for serving with the pork cheeks.

Add blackcurrants at the last minute, just before serving.

Serve the pork cheeks with a nice dollop of polenta, green beans and cress sprinkled on top. Serve as a hearty main course with good bread. Braised dishes are usually most popular in winter, but you can eat them all year round, especially if you, as with this dish, add the flavour of summer in the shape of berries, fresh greens and a touch of sharpness such as cress.

POLENTA

500 ml water
coarse salt
3 tbsp. good olive oil
100 g polenta (maize flakes)
100 ml semi-skimmed milk
50 g freshly grated Parmesan
1 lemon
sea salt
freshly ground pepper

Bring a saucepan with water, salt and oil to the boil and then sprinkle in the polenta while stirring, making sure it doesn't turn lumpy.

Cook at low heat for 10–15 minutes, until it turns into a thick porridge and remember to keep stirring, so it doesn't burn.

When the polenta is ready, add milk, grated Parmesan and lemon juice, which will give it a softer texture (more like oatmeal porridge). Add salt and pepper to taste.

1 kg pork cheeks
2 tbsp. good olive oil
2 carrots
2 shallots
1 garlic clove
5 thyme twigs
200 ml dark beer
400 ml good quality apple juice
sea salt
freshly ground pepper
500 ml chicken or calf's stock
300 g green beans
100 g fresh, de-stalked blackcurrants
1 tray of cress

Grilled fillet of pork

WITH MASHED POTATOES, WILD MUSHROOMS AND LEMON

4 people

1 fillet of pork (approx. 600–700 g)
sea salt
10 thyme sprigs
50–100 ml good olive oil
200 g wild mushrooms such as chanterelles and boletuses
1 kg small potatoes, preferably new potatoes
100 ml natural yoghurt
1 unwaxed lemon
freshly ground pepper
1 bunch or pot of watercress

Remove any remaining membranes or fat from the fillet of pork.

Cut the fillet into 4–8 smaller steaks and place in a dish. Sprinkle with salt and coarsely chopped thyme. Drizzle a little olive oil on top and leave to absorb the flavours for 15–20 minutes.

Clean the mushrooms and cut into smaller pieces, ready for frying.

Scrub the potatoes to get rid of any remaining earth and add to a saucepan with water and salt. Bring to the boil and leave to cook for approx. 15 minutes, until done but still firm.

Drain water from the potatoes and leave in the saucepan to cool off for a few minutes.

Crush the potatoes with a fork or a whisk and add yoghurt, olive oil, finely grated lemon zest and lemon juice, salt and freshly ground pepper to taste and make sure the mash is soft, yet chunky.

Grill the fillet steaks under a hot grill or on a grill pan for 3–4 minutes on each side, until they get a nicely burned surface, with a slightly pink and succulent middle. (You can also fry them on a regular frying pan.)

Fry the mushrooms in a little olive oil, on a hot frying pan, for a few minutes, until they collapse a little. Add salt and pepper to taste.

Serve the grilled fillet of pork with a nice dollop of potato compote, the fried mushrooms and watercress on top. Serve for lunch on its own or dinner with a fresh green salad and bread.

Pork rashers

4 people

Beat the pork rashers lightly with your hand, to flatten them. Then place them on a baking rack and sprinkle with coarse sea salt.

Place the baking rack in the oven with a roasting tray underneath to catch the fat that drips off the pork while roasting. Roast the pork rashers for approx. 15–20 minutes at 180°, until golden and crispy.

Peel the parsley roots and coarsely chop them. Peel the shallots and slice them finely.

Add parsley roots, onions and thyme to a saucepan with 3–4 tbsp. of the fat from the pork rashers, and add salt and pepper to taste. Cook onions and parsley roots on low heat for 7–8 minutes, until they start to caramelize and take colour.

Quarter the apples and remove core. Then dice coarsely. Add the apples to the saucepan and leave it all to cook for another 7–8 minutes, until the apples become soft, and it turns into thick compote.

Add grated lemon zest and lemon juice to the saucepan to taste before taking it off the heat.

Serve the apple and parsley root mash with rashers of pork, nice rye bread and maybe even a little strong mustard.

Serve as a hearty lunch dish or as a main course with boiled potatoes.

You can also make the mash without pork rashers, simply use butter instead of pork fat. And you can use celeriac, parsnip, Jerusalem artichoke, beetroot – or basically any other root vegetable – instead of parsley roots. You can serve the compote as a side dish with fried, grilled or baked fish.

800 g thick cut pork rashers
sea salt
400 g parsley roots (often called Hamburg parsley, parsnips can also be used instead)
4 shallots
5 thyme sprigs
freshly ground pepper
4 apples
1 unwaxed lemon

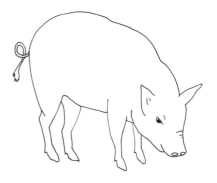

LAMB

Some people argue that lamb tastes of wool, which is why they won't eat it. It's a myth. And it's my claim that if you buy decent quality lamb, it'll be mild and delicate in taste and most people will actually appreciate it.

In the old days, spring would be considered the lamb season, but these days, lamb is available almost all year round. Lamb meat can vary a little in terms of colour, depending on breed and age, but you should always go for meat with a lovely, slightly pink colour as well as white, firm and dry fat. The meat must be firm and supple, and it should smell like meat – not wool!

You can grill, roast, braise, chop and make sausages out of lamb's meat, depending on which cut you buy. A good rule of thumb is that front cuts (throat, shank, neck and shoulder) take a long time to cook, and you should braise, slow roast or boil it. While cuts from the back of the beast, where you'll find the more supple pieces (back and legs), need short and precise cooking.

Roasted lamb rump

WITH BEANS, SPRING ONIONS,
MINI ROMAINE LETTUCE AND PARSLEY

4 people

2 rumps of lamb
5 thyme sprigs
2 garlic cloves
sea salt
freshly ground pepper
12 spring onions
100 g green beans
2 mini romaine lettuce
20 g butter
½ bunch of flat leaf parsley
½ unwaxed lemon

Remove any remaining membranes and most of the fat on the lamb rumps (leave a little fat, as it adds lovely flavour to the meat and it's great for frying).

Heat a frying pan and add the lamb rumps, fatty side down, as well as thyme and the whole garlic cloves. Brown the rumps well on both sides and them place them in an ovenproof dish. Add salt and freshly ground pepper to taste.

Roast the rumps in the oven for 8–10 minutes at 180°, leaving them vaguely pink in the middle.

Take the rumps out of the oven and leave to settle for 5–10 minutes before slicing them.

Top and tail both spring onions and green beans before rinsing in cold water. Chop the beans into small pieces.

Add butter to a sauté pan and heat until it melts. Add whole spring onions and chopped green beans and leave to sauté for a couple of minutes, allowing the vegetables to absorb the butter and soften.

Rinse the mini romaine and parsley and drain both in a colander. Cut the mini romaine into coarse chunks and shred the parsley.

Add the mini romaine and parsley to the sauté pan and toss well. Add salt, freshly ground pepper and lemon zest to taste.

Take the sauté pan off the heat, ensuring that the vegetables are not overcooked – think of it as a warm salad, with lots of freshness and crunchiness.

Slice the lamb rumps and serve with the warm salad on top.

Serve as a light lunch dish or a lovely summery main course with boiled new potatoes and bread. You can also grill the lamb rumps.

Open sandwich
on rye bread

4-5 fillets of lamb
150 g coarse salt
150g muscovado sugar
10 g coriander seeds
10 g juniper berries
5 g whole black peppercorns
10 g fennel seeds
5 g dill seeds
10 g green anise

4 people

1 carrot
1-2 new beetroots (keep the leaves)
2 tbsp. cider vinegar
2 tbsp. good rapeseed oil
1 tsp. liquid honey
sea salt
freshly ground pepper
4 slices of good quality rye bread
2 tbsp. fresh cheese (goat's cheese or any cream cheese is a good choice)
2 finely sliced marinated lamb fillets
½ bunch of tarragon

Peel the carrot and beetroots (keep the beetroot leaves) and slice thinly – using a mandoline or a very sharp knife.

Add the beetroots to a bowl and marinate in vinegar, oil, honey, salt and freshly ground pepper. Toss and leave for 5-10 minutes.

Spread the fresh cheese on the slices of rye bread before placing thin slices of marinated lamb fillet on top. Finally, top-up with the marinated beetroot salad, chopped tarragon and beetroot leaves.

MARINATED LAMB FILLET
8-10 people

Day 1

Remove membranes from lamb fillets before placing them in a deep dish.

Mix salt, muscovado sugar and the spices and pour the mixture over the meat, completely covering the fillets. Cover the dish in cling film and place in fridge.

Leave the lamb fillets in the fridge for 2-3 days (at approx. 5°) and turn them over daily to ensure that they marinate evenly. It's important that the fillets stay covered in marinade.

Day 3/4

The fillets are properly marinated when firm and still red in the middle. Drain marinade and throw out, but keep the spices and crush them in a mortar.

Gently dry the lamb fillets with some kitchen tissue and roll them in the crushed spices. Leave them in the fridge for another 24 hours, though you shouldn't cover them in cling film this time round, allowing the surface to harden a little.

Day 4/5

Serve thinly sliced as a starter with a little salad, or a root vegetable mash and a mustard dressing made with a little oil, vinegar, honey and mustard.

Marinated fillets of lamb will keep for 10-12 days in the fridge, if well wrapped in cling film or in a container with a lid.

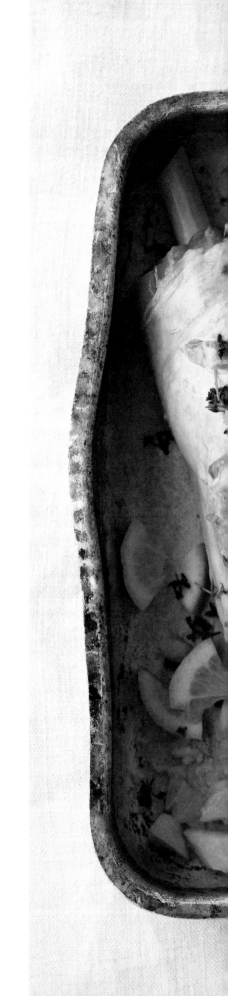

Slow Roasted Leg of Lamb
With preserved lemon and beer

Slow roasted leg of lamb

6–8 people

Score the leg of lamb and place in an ovenproof dish. Chop the thyme sprigs and cut the preserved lemon into large chunks. Rub the leg of lamb well with lemon, thyme, salt and freshly ground pepper.

Pour beer and water over and roast the leg of lamb in the oven for 3½ – 4 hours on a low heat of 130–140°C/250–275°F, until very tender. While roasting, it's important that you baste the meat with its juices at least two or three times.

Remove the leg of lamb from the oven and leave to sit for 10–15 minutes, before slicing it. Serve with the pan juices and the root vegetable salad with pear.

You can also serve the leg of lamb with potatoes or another salad. Or you can roast it the day before and serve cold.

1 leg of lamb
10 sprigs of thyme
1 preserved lemon (see recipe on page 145)
½ litre of brown ale, stout or bitter such as Guinness
3 ml water

SALAD OF ROOT VEGETABLES WITH PEAR

1 kg mixed root vegetables (carrots, parsley roots, turnips or celeriac)
4 pears
2 shallots
3–4 tbsp. cider vinegar
½ ml good olive oil
1 tbsp. liquid honey
2 tbsp. coarse mustard
sea salt
freshly ground pepper
1 bunch of flat leaf parsley

Peel the root vegetables and slice finely. Add to a bowl.

Quarter the pears and remove the core before slicing into thin wedges. Peel the shallots and slice finely.

Mix vinegar, oil, honey, mustard, salt and freshly ground pepper to make a dressing.

Toss the root vegetables, onion rings and pears with the dressing and sprinkle chopped parsley on top.

Rolled lamb sausage

APPLE AND FENNEL COMPOTE

3 apples
1 tbsp. cider vinegar
1 tbsp. sugar
10 fennel seeds
sea salt
freshly ground pepper
1 fennel bulb

Quarter the apples and remove core before chopping into bigger chunks.

Add the apple chunks to a saucepan and then add vinegar, sugar, fennel seeds, salt and freshly ground pepper. Place saucepan on the stove and bring to the boil.

Cook the apples for 8–10 minutes until they soften and turn into compote.

Take the apples off the heat and stir well – you should allow for some of the apple chunks to retain a little texture.

Add extra salt, pepper and vinegar to taste.

Finely chop the fennel and toss in with the apple compote. Leave the compote to cool down a little before serving.

12–14 people

Place the boneless piece of lamb on a chopping board, inner side up, and score lightly with a sharp knife, without penetrating the meat. Lightly beat the meat with a meat hammer or your hand, ensuring that it's completely flattened and its thickness even.

Pluck and chop the herbs (save the stalks for the brine). Quarter the apple and remove core before dicing it. Finely dice the fennel. Mix fennel, apple and herbs. Place the mixture on the lamb meat and add salt and freshly ground pepper to taste. Roll the meat tightly.

Tie some string tightly around the roll and make sure you close the ends properly, to ensure the filling stays put. Leave the roll in the fridge for 3–4 hours, allowing it to absorb the flavours of fruits and herbs, before cooking.

Add all ingredients for the brine to a saucepan; bring to the boil and add the roll of lamb. Simmer the roll for 1½ – 2 hours in a saucepan with a lid, over low heat. Make sure the roll is completely covered by the liquid at all times. You can place a small heatproof plate or bowl on top of the lamb roll to make sure it stays covered. Switch off the heat and leave the roll to sit for approx. 30 minutes, before taking it out and placing it between two baking sheets with something heavy on top. Leave until the lamb roll is cold.

Thinly slice the rolled lamb and serve with apple and fennel compote and rye bread.

1 – 1½ kg of boneless lamb
5 thyme sprigs
5 stalks of marjoram
5 stalks of bronze fennel
(alternatively fennel top, tarragon or chervil)
1 apple
1 fennel bulb
sea salt
freshly ground pepper

Brine for cooking the lamb
3 litres of water
330 ml lager
50 ml cider vinegar
10 whole black peppercorns
7–8 bay leaves
1–2 tbsp. coarse salt
stalks from the herbs

VENISON

In the past, venison has had a rather exclusive reputation, being hard to find outside the licensed game dealers who supply it wholesale. However, the world is waking up to the fact that venison is our most natural, organic and healthy meat, being very lean and low in fat.

So there's no reason why you shouldn't eat it more often, not least if you're lucky enough to go hunting yourself or if you know someone else who does. If not, you can always order some from your local butcher, although most good supermarkets now stock venison fillets, venison burgers and venison sausages, which are very popular indeed.

The hunting season for most venison is autumn and winter, and that's the time to eat deer, as it's both fresh and reasonably priced.

Saddle and legs are the most expensive cuts, but you usually pay less for shoulder, neck or breast meat. You can, for example, make venison ragout from both shoulder and neck; use the bones for making your own stock. Or you can mince some of the meat and make venison burgers.

When you buy venison from the butcher, you should always make sure that the meat is deeply red, and there should be no bullet wounds or coagulated blood. The surface should be slightly dry and there should be next to no fat.

Under no circumstances should you overcook venison, as it will become really dry and dull. But try as you go along, and don't be afraid to use some of the less classical cuts.

HUNTING SEASON
AUTUMN & WINTER
2014–15

01.09 – 31.01

Stag

01.10 – 31.01

Hind & Calf

01.09 – 31.01

Fallow Buck

01.10 – 31.01

Fallow Deer & Calf

01.09 – 31.01

Sika Stag

01.10 – 31.01

Sika Hind & Calf

16.05 – 15.07 & 01.10 – 31.01

Roebuk

01.10 – 31.01

Roe Deer & Lamb

Wild venison burgers

WITH PUMPKIN, CURLY KALE, PICKLED ONION SHELLS AND TARRAGON

4 people

2 onions
2 tbsp. cider vinegar
sea salt
20 g butter
½ Hokkaido pumpkin
300 g de-stalked curly kale
freshly ground pepper
600 g minced venison
½ bunch of tarragon

Peel the onions and add to a saucepan with just enough water to cover them.

Add vinegar, salt, half of the butter and bring to the boil. Cook for approx. 30 minutes. Then turn off the heat and leave to settle in the brine.

Split the Hokkaido pumpkin and peel one half (save the other half and use in a soup for example, see page 115). Scrape out the seeds.

Dice the pumpkin into squares of approx. 1 x 1 cm and add to a frying pan with the remaining butter. Gently fry the pumpkin squares, allowing them to absorb the butter and soften.

Rinse the curly kale well and leave to drain in a colander. Then chop coarsely.

Add the chopped kale to the pumpkin squares on the frying pan and leave to cook for a couple of minutes, until the kale collapses. Add salt and pepper to taste.

Take the boiled onions from the saucepan and halve them. Divide into individual shells. Add the onion shells to the frying pan. Toss everything well and add lots of chopped tarragon, salt and freshly ground pepper to taste.

Shape the minced venison into four steaks and fry them on a medium-hot frying pan in some olive oil for 3–4 minutes of both sides, until they get a nice and crunchy crust but remain slightly pink and succulent in the middle.

Serve as a main course with some potatoes and artisanal bread.

Venison broth

4–6 people

2 kg venison bones
(you can also use a poultry carcass)
approx. 3 litres of water
sea salt
¼ celeriac or some other white root
vegetable
1 carrot
2–3 tomatoes
1 onion
1 whole garlic
10 whole black peppercorns
2 juniper berries
3 bay leaves
5 thyme sprigs

Filling
2–300 g wild mushrooms
such as chanterelles and boletuses
2 tbsp. good olive oil
sea salt
freshly ground pepper
200 g Brussels sprouts
1 bunch of flat leaf parsley
100 g boiled grains
(whole barley, wheat or rye)

Chop bones/carcass into smaller bits. Place in the oven and roast hard for 15 minutes at 200°. Then add all bones to a saucepan, cover in water and bring to the boil. Skim the froth to avoid impurities, and than add some salt to rid the broth of any remaining impurities, before skimming off froth again. It is, however, important that you do not add too much salt, as you need to reduce the broth later on and it may become too salty.

Clean all vegetables and chop coarsely before adding to the broth. Then add herbs. Leave to simmer for 4–5 hours. If you leave the broth for too long, it might turn a little bitter. And if you give it too much heat, the liquid will turn cloudy.

Strain through a fine sieve into a clean saucepan and reduce the liquid a little to deepen the taste of venison. The broth is now ready to be served, but you can also use it in sauces or to braise venison on another occasion.

Clean the mushrooms and cut into smaller pieces. Then fry them in some olive oil on a hot frying pan for a couple of minutes, until they take colour and collapse a little. Add salt and pepper to taste.

Remove the outer leaves on the Brussels sprouts and throw them away. Then finely slice the sprouts and rinse in cold water.

Rinse the parsley and drain well before coarsely chopping.

Add all the ingredients to the broth and quickly re-heat, allowing it to heat up, yet not so much that the vegetables lose their freshness and crunchiness. Serve with good bread, either as a starter or as a main course – it's sufficiently filling. If you happen to have some cold, leftover venison, you can chop that into smaller bits and add to the broth as well.

Venison Ragout

with root vegetables, lingonberries and
celeriac mash

Venison ragout

4–6 people

600 g venison, without bones, fat and
membranes
(shoulder, neck or breast)
1 tbsp. good olive oil
3–4 shallots
3 carrots
3 parsley roots
2 turnips
5 thyme sprigs
1 garlic clove
4 whole juniper berries
sea salt
freshly ground pepper
330 ml dark beer
3 tbsp. cherry vinegar
or some other dark fruity vinegar
1 litre of venison or veal broth
20–25 g cold butter
1 bunch of flat leaf parsley

Remove any membranes from the venison and cut
into squares of approx. 2 x 2 cm. Brown the meat in
a saucepan with olive oil, over strong heat, giving
the pieces a nice crust on all sides.

Peel onions and root vegetables and cut into same
size as the meat. Add vegetables to the saucepan
along with thyme twigs, the garlic clove and lightly
crushed juniper berries and then brown until slightly
golden. Add salt and pepper to taste.

Add beer and vinegar to meat and vegetables and
reduce to half. Then add broth and bring to the boil.
Skim off froth to get rid of impurities, and leave to
simmer for approx. 1½ hours over low heat, until the
meat is tender.

Just before serving, add dollops of cold butter, which
will soften the taste of the ragout, adding a smooth
and delicious finish.

Add salt and pepper to taste and serve the ragout
with chopped parsley sprinkled on top along side
celeriac mash and speedily marinated lingonberries.

CELERIAC MASH

Peel the celeriac and quarter before adding to a saucepan. Cover in water with a little salt added.

Cook until tender, approx. 20 minutes, and then drain the water (you can save a little to adjust consistency of mash later).

Once you've drained the water, add the celeriac pieces to a food processor. Add double cream and finely grated lemon zest and lemon juice and blend until it becomes a coarse mash.

Add butter to a saucepan and heat gently, until it starts to foam and turn brown, giving off a slightly nutty scent, which goes really well with celeriac.

Pour the warm butter into the celeriac mash while the food processor is still on and blend until the mash is shiny and even. It should be a little softer than mashed potatoes. Add a little of the water you cooked the celeriac in if needed.

Add salt and pepper to taste.

1 celeriac
sea salt
50 ml double cream
1 unwaxed lemon
40 g butter
freshly ground pepper

QUICKLY MARINATED LINGONBERRIES

Add the fresh or frozen lingonberries to an ovenproof dish and sprinkle cane sugar on top.

Place in the oven and bake for 5–7 minutes at 160°, just long enough for the berries to get warm, absorb the sugar and collapse a little.

Remove berries from oven and leave to cool in the dish, which will allow them to retain some structure.

Add the berries to a bowl and serve with the ragout or other dishes with venison and other dark meats.

You can also put the lingonberries in a preserving jar and keep in the fridge for later use. Unopened, they'll keep for 30–40 days in the fridge. Once opened, they'll keep for 10–15 days.

200 g fresh or frozen lingonberries
(or cranberries)
4–5 tbsp. cane sugar

Grilled venison steak

4 people

Remove any membranes and fat from the fillet and cut into 8 smaller steaks. Put the steaks on a dish and place in the fridge until you want to grill them.

Rinse the scorzoneras well; they're usually covered in a great deal of earth. Peel and then add to a bowl with cold water and juice from half a lemon, which will prevent them from turning brown.

Peel the red onion; then halve it before slicing it finely. Add the strips of onion to a bowl and marinate with vinegar, honey and a little salt. Leave for 20–25 minutes, allowing the onion to soften a little and lose some of the sharp onion taste.

Quarter the apples and remove the core before cutting into large wedges.

Toss the steaks in some olive oil and grill on a hot grill pan or a barbeque for approx. 3–4 minutes on either side, giving them a nice and crispy surface with a rosy and succulent middle. Add salt and freshly ground pepper to taste.

Take the steaks off the pan and leave to settle for a couple of minutes before cutting.

Chop the scorzoneras into smaller chunks and fry them in butter on a frying pan for a couple of minutes, ensuring they turn a brown-golden colour with a crispy surface while also retaining a little bite. Add salt and freshly ground pepper to taste.

Remove the pan from the heat and add red onion and apples. Toss a few times and it's ready to serve with the steaks.

Halve the steaks and serve on a plate with scorzoneras, apples and onion on top. Add salt and pepper to taste and sprinkle some finely chopped herbs or kale over everything.

Serve as a lunch dish or as a main course with potatoes and bread.

800 g fillet of venison
1 kg scorzonera tubers
(black salsify)
½ lemon
1 red onion
2–3 tbsp. cider vinegar
1 tsp. liquid honey
sea salt
2 apples
3–4 tbsp. good olive oil
freshly ground pepper
10 g butter
1 handful herbs or a little kale
(curly or palm)

LIQUIDS

I really love collecting, picking and harvesting raw produce in season, when everything is at its best in terms of smell, looks, consistency, complexity and not least taste. And most often, I'll then use whatever I bring home to cook a great meal straight away. But preserving produce in jars, containers and bottles gives me almost an equal amount of pleasure. Opening a jar of preserved berries or fruit on a cold winter's day will bring back the scent of summer in a flash.

Use the abundance of berries, vegetables, fruit, herbs and nuts when they're in season.

Bottle them, or put them in jars or liquidize them by making schnapps, vinegar, syrup, vodka or whatever else takes your fancy. You can also check out #gemsommertilvinter (save summer for winter) or #gemvintertilsommer (save winter for summer).

Plum syrup

Approx. 600–700 ml

500 g plums
300 g sugar
½ lemon
1 litre of water
10 whole black peppercorns

Rinse the plums and add to a saucepan with sugar, juice from ½ lemon, water and peppercorns.

Bring to the boil and cook for 10–15 minutes over low heat. Turn the heat off and leave the plums to settle for another 10 minutes.

Then drain the plums (and save them for later. You can enjoy them with ice cream, on top of yoghurt or remove the stones, crush and use for jam) and pour the plum juice into another saucepan.

Heat and reduce juice to approx. half, as it starts to thicken and become syrupy.

Take the saucepan off the heat and pour the syrup into preserving jars or a bottle.

The syrup is lovely on top of yoghurt, porridge, berries, ice cream and cakes. It can also be used in dressings, salads as well as with baked and roasted vegetables.

Dandelion vinegar

1 preserving jar of approx. 1½ litres

4–5 handfuls of dandelions
1 litre of cider vinegar

Add the dandelions to a preserving jar or an airtight container.

Pour the vinegar over dandelions and leave to marinate for at least 3 days in the fridge before using. If stored in a cool place, the dandelions will keep for up to 6 months.

Marinated dandelions are wonderful as garnish with roast meat, poultry or grilled fish. The vinegar gets a perfumed flowery taste, a bit more 'green' and grass-like than the rose hip vinegar. Use in dressings and marinades and with both raw and baked vegetables.

Marinated rosehip leaves

1 preserving jar of approx. 1½ litres

2–3 handfuls of rosehip leaves
1 litre of cider vinegar

Add the rosehip leaves to a preserving jar or an airtight container.

Pour vinegar over rosehip leaves and leave to marinate for at least 3 days in the fridge before using. If stored in a cool place, the rosehip leaves will keep for up to 6 months.

Marinated rosehip leaves are wonderful as a garnish with roast meat, poultry or grilled fish. You can also use the leaves with ice cream or in desserts, jams and juices to add a touch of summer. The vinegar gets a perfumed flowery taste and works wonders in dressings and marinades.

Cherry schnapps

Approx. 1 litre

20 fresh cherries
4 whole roots of liquorice
1 tbsp. sugar
1 bottle of neutral schnapps
(750 ml)
2 empty bottles

Make small cuts in the cherries and divide into both empty bottles.

Gently bash the liquorice roots, which will open them a little, and add to the bottles. Then divide sugar and schnapps into both bottles. Put a lid on the bottles and shake gently.

Store the schnapps somewhere dark and cool for at least 3–4 weeks before drinking.

The cherry schnapps makes for a nice change from regular schnapps around Christmas, but you can also enjoy it warm as a liqueur with cheese and dessert.

Rhubarb vodka

Approx. 1 litre

3–4 small stalks of rhubarb
3–4 geranium stalks
2 tbsp. sugar
1 bottle of plain vodka (700–750 ml)
2 empty bottles

Divide the rhubarb and geranium stalks between the two empty bottles. If the rhubarb stalks are too large for the bottles, cut them into smaller pieces.

Pour in vodka and then put a lid on the bottles and shake gently.

Leave the vodka to settle somewhere dark and cool for at least 3–4 weeks before drinking.

Enjoy the vodka with an ice cube or mix with champagne, prosecco or cold white wine as an aperitif.

You can also use berries and fruits as well as herbs such as verbena, lemon balm or mint.

Taste the food, until the flavour is there!

Regardless of whether you're spending hours cooking a sophisticated stew or you're just making a simple salad, tasting is of the essence, and preferably more than once. It's important that you make sure you get the right taste. (Fortunately) taste is individual, which is why you always have to taste as you go along to find the right balance between sweet, sour and salt – for you.

If the recipe says plum vinegar, you might think you can only make this dish with plum vinegar. However, in most cases, it's merely important that you add something acidic, which will add freshness to the dish. Don't be intimidated by what a recipe says, but think about what the dish might lack, and then use whatever is available.

ICING SUGAR

SUGAR

HONEY

Sweet

DRIED FRUIT

SYRUP

FRUIT JUICE

SOFT BROWN SUGAR

SOUR PICKLE

CAPERS

WINE

Sour

VINEGAR

LIME

GRAPE

LEMON

FISH SAUCE

ANCHOVIES

SOY SAUCE

Salt

CAPERS

OYSTERS

SALT

CAYENNE PEPPER

MUSTARD

PEPPER

Hot

CURRY

HORSERADISH

CHILLI

Index

Thank You

Anders Schønnemann for your time, commitment, sparring, your beautiful photos and your friendship!

Sweet sister Sidsel for finding all the beautiful items for the book, for your ideas and creativity and for taking the time and effort to make the wonderful drawings.

Mother Anni who initiated my interest in cooking and supported me in my career.

Father Bjarne for letting me use his beach, and for fetching a primus stove and holding the ladder.

Father-in-law Jens for inspiration for drawings.

Trine Ravn for believing in this project and making it possible

Marie Holm for making my texts and recipes comprehensible.

Morten Buch Lassen for the book's beautiful graphic design and for sticking with many of your numerous ideas.

Claus Meyer for words, time and inspiration over many years.

Mikkel and Louise for your interest, ideas and empathy.

Charlotte, Kasper, Jesper, Ramana, Jakob, Alekandra and everyone else at Hjorten for your understanding, patience and support for this project.

Gurli Elbækgaard, Julie Bonde Bulck, Birgitte Due Madsen, Nina, Susanne and Peter for lending me so many lovely things.

My beautiful wife Camilla and our lovely children, Oscar, Alma, Konrad and Viggo, this one's for you, because you're always there for me, supporting and believing in me no matter the madness I get involved in … I love you!

Mikkel Karstad

Mikkel Karstad (born 1973) is a chef, food columnist, and former gastronomic advisor to Claus Meyer. For a number of years, Mikkel worked in the kitchens of several Michelin-rated restaurants in Copenhagen, and he has also worked as a food stylist on a number of cookbooks, including Claus Meyer's giant 'Almanac'. Mikkel writes about food for magazines such as Gastro, Euroman and Mad & Bolig (Food & Home), and simultaneously, he blogs on weyouteyate.com where he shares his favourite recipes and raw produce.

Anders Schønnemann

Anders Schønnemann (born 1974) is a photographer who specializes in food and interiors. Originally, Anders wanted to be a chef, but then he discovered that his love of food could just as easily be expressed by way of photography. When Anders is not engaged in taking photos for cookbooks by Claus Meyer, Morten Heiberg and Mikkel Karstad, he works for international magazines such as Jamie Magazine, Kinfolk and Vanity Fair and other clients including Gordon Ramsay while the Mandarin Oriental Hotels also benefit from his simple, Scandinavian style.

Oven Temperature Conversion Table

Use this table as a guideline when converting cooking temperatures between celcius, fahrenheit, gas and fan ovens:

Gas	°F	°C	Fan
1	275	140	120
2	300	150	130
3	325	170	150
4	350	180	160
5	375	190	170
6	400	200	180
7	425	220	200
8	450	230	210
9	475	240	220

Imperial to Metric Conversion Table

Use this table as a guideline when converting imperial measurements to metric.
1 pound (lb) = 16 ounces
1 kilo (kilogram / kilo) = 1000g

½ oz	10 g	6 oz	175 g
¾ oz	20 g	7 oz	200 g
1 oz	25 g	8 oz	225 g
1½ oz	40 g	9 oz	250 g
2 oz	50 g	10 oz	275 g
2½ oz	60 g	12 oz	350 g
3 oz	75 g	1 lb	450 g
4 oz	110 g	1 lb 8 oz	700 g
4½ oz	125 g	2 lb	900 g
5 oz	150 g	3 lb	1.35 kg

US Cups Conversion Table

If you would like to use the American "cups" method of measurement, the table below can be used as a conversion guideline for non-liquid ingredients.

Officially, a US Cup is 240ml (or 8.45 imperial fluid ounces.) This is slightly different from an Australian, Canadian and South African Cup which is 250ml. As long as you use the same cup for measuring out each of your ingredients, the proportions should work out the same.

Ingredient	1 cup	¾ cup	⅔ cup	½ cup	⅓ cup	¼ cup	2 tbsp
Flour	120g	90g	80g	60g	40g	30g	15g
Flour (sieved)	110g	80g	70g	55g	35g	27g	13g
Sugar (granulated)	200g	150g	130g	100g	65g	50g	25g
Icing Sugar	100g	75g	70g	50g	35g	25g	13g
Brown Sugar	180g	135g	120g	90g	60g	45g	23g
Cornflour (corn starch)	120g	90g	80g	60g	40g	30g	15g
Rice (uncooked)	190g	140g	125g	95g	65g	48g	24g
Couscous (uncooked)	180g	135g	120g	90g	60g	45g	22g
Oats (uncooked)	90g	65g	60g	45g	30g	22g	11g
Table Salt	300g	230g	200g	150g	100g	75g	40g
Butter	240g	180g	160g	120g	80g	60g	30g
Vegetable Shortening	190g	140g	125g	95g	65g	48g	24g
Nuts (chopped)	150g	110g	100g	75g	50g	40g	20g
Nuts (ground)	120g	90g	80g	60g	40g	30g	15g
Breadcrumbs (fresh)	60g	45g	40g	30g	20g	15g	10g
Breadcrumbs (dry)	150g	110g	100g	75g	50g	40g	20g
Sultanas / Raisins	200g	150g	130g	100g	65g	50g	22g

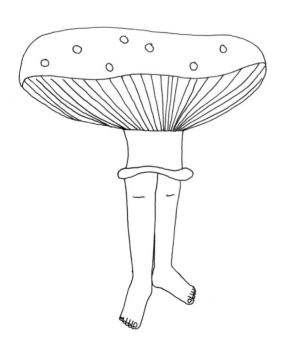

Coøk

Published in the UK in 2015 by Clearview Books
22 Clarendon Gardens, London W9 1AZ
www.clearviewbooks.com

First published in Danish by
Lindhardt og Ringhof Forlag A/S, 2014

A CIP record of this book is available from the
British Library

ISBN 978 1 908337 245

English translation: IP Words v/Iben Philipsen
Production: Simonne Waud
Copy editor: Catharine Snow

Printed in China